ON A WEDNESDAY NIGHT

poems from the creative writing workshop
at the university of new orleans

University of New Orleans Press
Manufactured in the United States of America

ISBN: 978-1-60801-171-1

Cover design: Donna Guillory
Book design: Alex Dimeff

UNIVERSITY OF NEW ORLEANS PRESS
unopress.org

ON A WEDNESDAY NIGHT

poems from the creative writing workshop
at the university of new orleans

edited by Kay Murphy

Poems by Graduates and Faculty of the Creative Writing Workshop Celebrating Twenty-five Years of the Master of Fine Arts Writing Program at the University of New Orleans

for my Daughter
Melissa

The editor would like to thank:

John Gery for rounding up more students and poems and for providing the list of poets who have visited the CWW

Jessica Morey-Collins for her early work on this project

Nicole Boyer and Donna Guillory for their tireless and meticulous proofreading

Donna Guillory for expressing in art exactly what I wanted for the cover

—Kay Murphy

CONTENTS

faculty poems

Editor's Preface

Kay Murphy

The Creative Writing Workshop (CWW) was struggled into existence by a handful of warrior writers in 1990. The history of this ultimate victory is detailed in John Gery's comprehensive introduction to this anthology. In 2016 a volume of fiction by graduates and faculty was published which celebrates the 25th anniversary of the program. This volume of poetry celebrates the 25th anniversary of the first graduates of the Workshop in 1994. A poem and song lyric are included from the first graduate class by poet and musician, Jim McCormick.

Most editors of national poetry anthologies solicit poems from friends and well-known poets and later regret that due to limits of space many deserving poets do not appear in the anthology. I make no such claim. My objective from the beginning was to be inclusive. I wanted every poet who graduated from the CWW and Low Res program to be represented by at least one poem. If the poet graduated from our rigorous workshops, then they certainly have poems worth publishing in this volume. I sent out submission guidelines every three months for the first year, extending the deadline each time. I sent emails to poets I knew, posted Facebook announcements, made phone calls, sent texts, and urged every poet to spread the word. However, for reasons unknown, many poets who were contacted were unable to send poems and others were not reached by my efforts. That is what I regret.

However, every poet who submitted work has at least one poem included.

The choices were sometimes difficult because they often did not send poems that I mentored and that have changed my life and my sometimes unyielding notion of what a poem should or should not be. But what I like or do not like in a poem is not a basis for accepting or rejecting it. Therefore, the poems included here are the ones the students want to be represented by. This is their anthology, not mine.

I am heartened by the number of poems that honor our city. Whether their makers are natives or transplants, they have been taken in by its magic, and by its violence. Several elegies are included which memorialize both the deaths of local citizens who were murdered and those who died of natural causes, such as our beloved Chair, John Cooke.

Since my workshops were mostly experiments into received forms, I am also reassured that my belief in the importance of practicing such forms are a necessity to understand free verse is strengthened by the number and variety of forms, both traditional and experimental: the sestina, pantoum, sonnet crown, terza rima, villanelle, iambic pentameter, blank verse, cento, ekphrastic, prose poem, concrete poetry, and a selection of experimental nonce forms by both students and faculty. The diction is not limited to American vernacular but includes examples of Latin, German, French, Russian, Arabic, and Spanish which testifies to the international awareness of our students, many of whom live and teach in other countries.

In short, it was an honor to be asked to edit this anthology, and a pleasure to reconnect with students, to read again poems that I love, to be introduced to new work, and to know that the dedication and perspiration of the CWW faculty continue to inspire our students long after graduation.

Losar, 5 February 2019

A Brief History of Poetry Writing at University of New Orleans

John Gery

The history of poetry and poetry writing at the University of New Orleans necessarily begins with the poet among the university's founding faculty, K. Raeburn Miller. His story as I heard it goes that Miller, a native of Travis, Texas, who had studied with poet Donald Justice at the famed Iowa Writers Workshop in the 1950s – where he earned both MA and MFA degrees and had assisted Justice in editing the *Collected Poems of Weldon Kees* (an American classic text still in print) – had come to New Orleans from Austin around 1960 to visit to a friend. At the time Miller was working as a certified public accountant since, as for most poets, employment in his own field was nearly impossible to find. However, during his visit his friend apparently mentioned that Louisiana State University in Baton Rouge had just opened a branch campus on the grounds of the recently abandoned Naval Air Station on the shore of Lake Pontchartrain, and might not Miller check into whether the new school might need a poet.

This chance opportunity initiated what has become the surprising history of poetry at UNO, resulting almost sixty years later in this rich collection of diverse poetry by graduates from the last twenty-five years of UNO's Master of Fine Arts program in Creative Writing. In fact, not only did Miller secure a position in English under the administration of UNO's first chancellor, Homer Hitt, but (among other unexpected tasks) he became instrumental in designing the university curricula, as well as establishing the English department with his fellow pioneers George Reinecke, Seraphia Leyda, Cooper Mackin, Cresap Watson, Malcolm Magaw, Robert Gibbons, Kenneth Holditch, Gordon Fleming, Ed Socola, Rima Reck, Gordon Fleming, Vernon Torczon, Viron Barnhill, Carol Gelderman, Donald Schuler, and others. In truth, as a poet, Miller was socially uncomfortable as a professor or colleague (at least when I knew him), yet he devoted himself to the university's academic growth and to his own poems – gathered in his collection, *Millenary* (1986), published by Maxine Cassin's New Orleans Poetry Journal Press, and later after his untimely death in 1990, in his collected volume, *The Comma After Love: Selected Poems of Raeburn Miller* (1994, edited by Donald Justice, Cooper R. Mackin, Kay Murphy, and Richard D. Olson), published by University of Akron Press, whose poetry editor, Elton Glaser, was one of Miller's earliest students to achieve success as a poet himself.

To say Miller had a retiring personality is an understatement, as even as Chair of English and (later) as Associate Dean of the Graduate School, he often retreated behind his closed office door at noon, preferring to eat his lunch alone. Still, he had untiring energy, it seemed, for finding and attracting writers, especially poets, from around the U.S. to come to New Orleans and teach at UNO. Despite his palpable shyness in most of his professional (and probably all of his personal) interactions, he was shameless about seeking poets and inducing them to accept temporary teaching jobs at UNO in the 1970s when, because of the national energy crisis that increased demand for Louisiana oil, the university was growing rapidly in student population. To be sure, all the young faculty who later proposed, designed, and developed Creative Writing eventually into one of the more diverse, dynamic, and unpredictable Masters programs in the South, if not in the U.S., were originally hired (as temporary instructors, no less) by Miller – fiction writers Joanna Leake, James Knudsen, and Rick Barton, and me. Miller and his close colleague, Seraphia Leyda, had also hired younger professors who later aided and abetted the writers' insurgency – most notably, John Cooke and Robert Burdette, as well as Elizabeth Penfield who, as chair later, worked to create permanent positions for these writers.

The rocky institutional start of Creative Writing as an academic discipline here has been recounted elsewhere, most ably by the soulful novelist Rick Barton and by departmental historian Robert Shenk. But within the genre of poetry, which, after all, was Miller's first love, the list of poets he hired reads almost as a sample Who's Who among younger American poets of the era: Everette Maddox, Nikki Stiller, Jeanie Thompson, Carolyne Wright, David Wojahn, Gillian Conoley, Joel Dailey, Yusef Komunyakaa, Caroline Maisel, Katherine Soniat, David Franks, Gordon Anderson, Elizabeth

Thomas, Kay Murphy, William Oandasan, Richard Katrovas, Ralph Adamo, James Hietter, and others I have undoubtedly forgotten – all within a four-year span! It was as though he divined it best to fill the hoppers with poets before the bottomless supply of them would get cut off by budget cuts, which, in fact, started to hit hard by the mid-1980s. As it was for their scholarly and other writing colleagues among the Instructors who came to fill more than half the positions in English by 1983, the teaching load was heavy and usually involved little instruction in poetry, let alone in poetry writing. Still, New Orleans proved an attractive city for itinerant poets, despite what struck some as the (then) barren Naval Air Station qua state university extension campus where classes were held in rudimentary buildings more reminiscent of a state prison ground – with its cement block walls, rows of doors leading onto outdoor balconies on the upper floors, linoleum floors, asbestos ceilings, posterboard walls, unwashed blackboards, and spider-webbed windows covered by dusty, industrial blinds—than an institution of higher learning.

When I first visited UNO from California, before accepting the job offer I had received, I made the grave, naive mistake of assuming that the photograph on the cover of the UNO catalogue of St. Louis Cathedral in Jackson Square was a picture of the university chapel! Upon arriving on campus, I immediately searched the grounds for the chapel but became disoriented and somewhat disheartened that nothing around me seemed remotely like it. But I took the job gratefully (at a salary of about $11,000) and came to acknowledge and embrace UNO's modest origins. Having found an affordable studio apartment in the French Quarter, when I first worked at UNO, I found myself at first commuting on the Elysian Fields bus, essentially taking an opposite route from that of Blanche DuBois on the Desire streetcar when she famously arrives from Laurel, Mississippi. Each day I'd leave behind the narrow streets, hidden courtyards, wrought iron balconies, sultry air, and dark taverns open all night in the "Quarters" for the (at the time) treeless, flat expanse of the campus, where the grounds in a downpour quickly turned, as they still do, into a swamp which the bulk of students must trudge through from class to class – and so to their cars, and so to their service jobs, much like Randall Jarrell's weary ticket taker in "The Woman at the Washington Zoo."

Nonetheless, although it was the era before the internet – indeed, before faculty had telephones in their offices (and before some even had offices!) – classes quickly filled with undergraduates especially eager to earn their degree, if not quite so eager for the education to go with it. And the challenge to the raft of young poets that Raeburn Miller had amassed by Lake Pontchartrain – together with the young, ambitious academics specializing in work ranging from Dante's numerology to the plays of Vaclav Havel, from Blake's vision of Satan to the variations in New Orleans dialect – was to entrance freshmen students not only to pass, but to engage in what they were learning. And I would hazard now that an inordinate percentage of those students, whether they actually passed their composition and literature courses or not, can probably today remember their English teachers, since they always had direct contact with them. Most of the writers who joined UNO may not have been natives of the Deep South (with notable exceptions, such as Rick Barton and Yusef Komunyakaa), but despite UNO's public reputation (that is, as having little or no reputation at all) and despite its sometimes questionable advertising campaigns by well-meaning but misguided administrators who have passed through over the years, its true reputation lies with its own alumni, who consistently characterize UNO as an academically demanding, substantive institution that challenges students regardless of their backgrounds and privileges (or lack thereof), and across campus it has been staffed by faculty whom poet Ed Dorn would likely dub "serious dudes!"

Although the 1980s passed without even an official vote taken whether to establish a fine arts degree in creative writing at UNO, during that decade members of the English department slowly put into place the courses needed later to create a full curriculum for an MFA degree – first, specialized genre courses in fiction and poetry writing at the undergraduate level, then similar graduate courses, then nonfiction writing and genre studies courses. This development required subtle maneuvering, especially by Barton, who (after being hired as tenure-track Assistant Professor over a tumultuous two-year period) quickly rose through the ranks of university administration, becoming a Freshman Coordinator, then Associate Dean of Liberal Arts, then Dean, and eventually University Provost, all the while regularly teaching fiction writing and, as importantly, working as a prolific writer not only as a novelist but as a film critic and essayist. By sheer institutional finesse (maybe because his life's partner, Joyce Dombourian, is an accomplished lawyer?), Barton garnered the support of his creative writing colleagues and others in the administration (particularly the English Chair John Cooke, Acting Dean of Liberal Arts Kevin Graves, and Dean of the Graduate School Robert Cashner,) and connived under the radar to pull off the unheard-of miracle of launching an MFA Creative Writing program in New Orleans without the anticipated resistance of the LSU Board of Supervisors. UNO's MFA in Creative Writing was proposed as an interdisciplinary degree to be shared by two Liberal Arts departments, with fiction and poetry in English and playwriting and screenwriting in what was then Drama and Communications. The designers foresaw it then – and it remains now – unique in the field for its multi-genre range, first including four genres, then expanding soon after to include creative nonfiction writing, which brought onto the MFA faculty both longtime UNO faculty – mainly, the eminent literary biographer Carol Gelderman, an LSU Distinguished Professor, and the dapper fiction and jazz critic John Cooke – and then new faculty, at first, Miles Harvey for a year, then in 1999, the Mississippi native, Randy Bates, author of the widely praised memoir on a New Orleans boxer, RINGS: On the Life and Family of Collis Phillips, among other timely works often exploring the difficult personal circumstances of the Civil Rights era in the Deep South.

Among poets on staff, even before the degree was approved, three poets—Cynthia Hogue (who had been hired after Raeburn Miller's sudden death from a stroke in 1990), Richard Katrovas, and I—were already offering graduate courses in poetry writing and directing occasional theses under the option in Creative Writing within the English Masters. Still, even before the ink on the MFA degree papers was dry and the "program" opened its doors in 1990, poets and other writers flooded the Liberal Arts building to enroll, so that by 1994 UNO awarded its first MFA diplomas to, among other writers, four poets – Irvin (Chris) Christopher, James McCormick, Lara Tucker, and Lisa van der Linden. All four had successfully initiated the as-yet untested institutional process of passing a Masters comprehensive exam in Poetry Writing and completing a volume of original poems. When Hogue, Katrovas, and I met early on to devise guidelines for each student's thesis year, we hammered out the basic plan MFA poets must contend with today of following a rigorous process of submitting individual poems, sections of a sequence, or other clusters to their chosen thesis director and spending the better part of a year revising, rescinding, reworking, re-inventing, rebutting and re-ordering their poems into a polished half-book-length collection of works – a requirement for length we agreed upon as a better choice than to ask students to write a half-polished full-length collection. In addition, the comprehensive exam for poets consists of two sections: the development of a literature course introducing college students to the genre of poetry, complete with a syllabus and a pedagogical statement, and a timed exam analyzing poems in a packet assembled by MFA faculty and distributed two weeks prior to the comprehensive exam date.

However, not long after the degree was fully in place, by 1995, the talented and formidable poet Cynthia Hogue was hired to direct the Stadler Poetry Center at Bucknell University in Pennsylvania, among the most distinguished poetry centers in U.S., and soon after, with some controversy and the introduction of UNO's Low Residency MFA degree in Creative Writing, Richard Katrovas departed New Orleans first to administer UNO's Prague summer program, then for a similar position at Western Michigan University. So for a brief time I was the sole poet on the MFA faculty in New Orleans. But as quickly as the line for a poet's position could be approved through the LSU system channels, in 1999 Kay Murphy (who had already been teaching poetry writing as an Instructor at every level, including for the MFA, since her arrival in 1984) was hired as an Assistant Professor.

For the next fourteen years, until her retirement in 2013, Murphy and I worked hard together to create stability and continuity for graduate student poets and to maintain high artistic standards. Murphy brought a rare combination of talent, experience, and expertise that has had a profound impact on UNO's legacy. She fought determinedly to educate herself as an adult and earned her MFA degree in poetry writing at Goddard College's—later Warren Wilson College's—groundbreaking low-residency program before such programs became as prominent as they are now. So without pomp she serves as a role model for the majority of UNO's graduate poets, who often find themselves also facing the struggles of studying and writing poetry in the face of adversity, not as a luxury or artistic choice, but as a calling, a necessity for survival. Yet as both a poet and a teacher, Murphy is a disciplined formalist who demands that her students become conversant in traditional literary technique sufficient to bring that knowledge and facility to their own work, even if they do not choose ultimately to write such verse themselves. There's nothing "touchy-feely" about a creative writing class with Kay Murphy, yet the drives and fears that compel poets to practice their art are always on the line in her seminars. For her, whether in her own work or in her assessment of that of her students, art, imagination, and candor weigh equally in the making of a poem. Throughout this collection, poems may display their inventiveness or cunning, but few if any rely on mere cleverness for their effects, as they bear the mark of Kay Murphy's wisdom.

By the end of its first decade, while admittedly appearing as not much more than a blip on the expanding national scene of MFA programs in creative writing, UNO's program stabilized nonetheless, attracting an increasingly diverse set of student poets who have always varied greatly by background, ethnicity, age, race, sexual orientation, and especially artistic sensibility. An incoming class typically might consist of poets ranging in age from twenty-one to seventy or older. At the turn of the millennium, UNO further embarked on becoming one of the first MFA programs to offer a "Low Residency" degree, taking advantage of the ever-increasing presence of the internet to explore and devise a curricula that allowed writers worldwide, regardless of their circumstances, to enroll in "online" courses in writing and literature, while spending a month in the summer to travel to varying locations, mostly in Europe, for intensive workshops and literature courses geared specifically to them. At first, the courses were held at Charles University in Prague under Richard Katrovas's directorship, but poet Bill Lavender, an early UNO MFA alumnus, was soon hired to administer the Low Residency (as well as to direct UNO Press), and he worked ferociously to build the program across the genres. In 2002, UNO signed on as the host of the Associated Writing Programs conference held in New Orleans, jettisoning the MFA into the national limelight, and in 2003 the Low Residency moved from Prague to Madrid for several years, as well as expanded to include other sites – especially for poets at the Ezra Pound Center for Literature at Brunnenburg, Italy, which I had founded in 1990, but also in Montpelier, France. Through Lavender's charismatic leadership and receptivity to poets and writers across the spectrum of literary styles, and through his hiring of an enthusiastic staff, the Low Residency grew to become a vital complementary component in UNO's writing program through the early 2000s, later migrating from Madrid to San Miguel de Allende, Mexico, for several years, then to Edinburgh, Scotland. Besides an international corps of students, the Low Res also numbered an impressive number of visiting poets to teach overseas—Peter Gizzi, Susan Schultz, Peter Thompson, and MFA alumna Shelley Puhak among them. After Lavender's departure, today the primary summer program is housed at the University of Cork, Ireland, but the Brunnenburg program continues drawing poets from the MFA as well as from throughout the world to study Pound's formidable work and poetry writing.

Besides its steady growth in student population through the first twenty years, the MFA degree (at first shunning the term "program" so as not to raise any hackles among those on the LSU System Board of Regents and any others who might object to the creative arts at UNO) continued to enrich life on campus, despite how many UNO students continued to commute from school to work to home, as they had from the university's beginning. Through the years, the poets and writers on staff have regularly offered a panoply of extracurricular activities and literary opportunities for those who wish to take advantage of them. As early as 1980, John Cooke applied for a state grant and invited me to work with him on the first version of the New Orleans Poetry Festival, held at UNO and throughout the city, featuring three prominent visiting poets, Robert Hass, Ellen Bryant Voigt, and Al Young. Over the years – again, despite a minimum and often nonexistent budget for visiting lecturers and writers – the wide range of remarkable poets who have spoken and worked with students at UNO is impressive. In 1990, thanks to a matching grant from the National Endowment for the Arts, Jim Knudsen and I created a semester-long program of weeklong residencies each that brought four writers to campus for extended stays that included readings, class visits, interviews, informal gatherings with students, and special events: Ishmael Reed, Denise Levertov, Alice McDermott, and Frederick Turner. McDermott spoke about working with director Milos Forman on the adaption of her novel for the screen; Read was glad to stir controversy as both a novelist and poet, challenging students, faculty, and administrators not only about their nascent racial prejudices, but their literary ones; Turner, probably the only American poet ever under contract to NASA, envisioned a near future where the cybernetics and other scientific developments would transform universities into dynamic agents in cultural change (as indeed has proven to be the case); and Levertov spoke forthrightly not only about the political responsibility of poets to engage in social change and human rights, but about the inherent conflict between what she considered the business of "networking" among poets seeking publication and the high standards essential for poetry as an art. In fact, the same week she visited as our last guest artist Levertov had been invited to a ceremony in New York to receive that year's prestigious Poet's Prize, but she declined the invitation because of her prior commitment to UNO. During her residency, in addition to her scheduled events on campus and in the city, she also attended Mass at St. Louis Cathedral and assisted in serving a meal at a soup kitchen. The dress she wore for her capstone reading she purchased at a second hand shop in Canal Street, yet she was eloquent for the reading, not only charming the university Chancellor but winning over a new generation of readers.

While for the faculty, the visits from so many distinguished poets accrue, most students only get to hear and meet a handful before they graduate and depart. I have found, later, that individuals recall with great clarity one or two specific poets who visited during their years who had a significant impact on them. Whether a visiting poet speaks well or blunders, their impact inevitably serves as students' introduction to the professional side of writing. Other opportunities that can work similarly have grown steadily over the years (again, despite an unchanging budget) through a variety of venues. While the student literary publication, *Ellipsis* (originally entitled *The Beachcomber*, in concert with other Lake Pontchartrain motifs dating from UNO's founding – the Privateers,

Jean Lafitte, "The Cove," Driftwood), usually publishes a strong sampling of students' poetry and has offered The Robert Gibbons Prize for the best poem accepted. By the early 1980s, thanks to an endowed gift in collaboration with the English department by Andrea Gereighty, a UNO MA alumna and active poet herself with Lee Grue's New Orleans Poetry Forum, we funded into perpetuity through the Academy of American Poets in New York the Andrea Saunders Gereighty Award, given each spring for a poem or group of poems selected by a distinguished poet outside UNO. Then in 1999, as a tribute to the stunning work by Texas poet Vassar Miller after her death the year before, her close friend from New Orleans, poet Maxine Cassin, initiated a poetry award in Miller's name specifically for UNO graduate student poets: The judges (from across the U.S.) are encouraged to select a poem or group of poems from those submitted not only for their craft and artistry, but for how they reflect (however broadly interpreted) Miller's unique ability as one who suffered her entire life from cerebral palsy to overcome adversity to produce poetry brilliant in design and deeply informed by her spirit. Then in 2010, after the deaths of both Maxine Cassin and her husband Joseph Cassin within three days of each other after a marriage of almost sixty years, their son, the talented cellist Danial Cassin, established the annual Maxine and Joseph Cassin Award for the Best MFA Thesis in Poetry. For undergraduates, in 2005, after the untimely death (at age thirty-two) of Ryan Chighizola, a talented poet and poetry scholar who earned his Masters at the Naropa Institute in Colorado, his classmate Amy D'Antonio and others collaborated with the Chighizola family to establish in his memory a generous scholarship for an undergraduate concentrating in poetry writing and poetry.

Further opportunities for MFA students outside classes have included participation in the Tennessee Williams Literary Festival, an unusual and popular New Orleans conference involving play performances, panel discussions, readings, and receptions that annually attracts directors, actors, filmmakers, academics, tourists, and who knows who else, as well as prominent writers, including over the years Williams's brother Dakin, Oscar-winning actress Kim Hunter, John Kennedy Toole's piano-playing mother, film critic Roger Ebert, actor Alec Baldwin, and other luminaries; the festival is also now concurrent with the New Orleans Saints and Sinners conference that brings some of the brightest stars in contemporary literature. Also in the spring many UNO poets take advantage of what has become a ritual retreat of MFA students and faculty to the Gulf Coast Association for Creative Writing Teachers meeting in Fairhope, Alabama, on the banks of Mobile Bay – a small but lively gathering where young poets can get a taste of a professional conference consisting of readings, panels, and keynote speakers and compete for student awards, but as important, where they can engage with their counterparts from other graduate writing programs from across the Gulf Coast from Miami to Houston. Another essential part of the MFA program that mixes poets with the other writers on campus is *Bayou*, UNO's literary journal staffed entirely by students under faculty supervision. Originally a joint project developed by Joanna Leake with the University of Western Florida, the MFA program now runs the journal entirely, which accepts submissions from any writer in the world except those affiliated with UNO. Run professionally, it provides students with firsthand experience in literary editing (including through its prominent online presence) published by UNO Press. Through the years, added to the assistantships, internships, and editorial positions available with *Bayou*, UNO Press, now under the directorship of resourceful and adventurous MFA alumnus in fiction, Abram Himmelstein, has also offered students both academic and volunteer positions to work closely with each stage of an academic press' production process, from soliciting and evaluating manuscripts that come across the transom to the hard work of the promotion and sales of books published not for their marketability but for what lies between their covers.

On the darker side, beginning with the sudden, sad death of Jim Knudsen in 2004, followed by the catastrophe of Hurricane Katrina in 2005 and the ever-shrinking budget allotment from the Louisiana legislature to health care and higher education the decade after that, and because of restrictions against hiring, the MFA needed to recover and renew itself for the twenty-first century. For poetry students in particular, we were unable to restore the position for a third poet on staff, which therefore intensified Murphy's and my workload in the graduate program, despite other obligations. Yet we were certainly aided, especially for staffing thesis committees, by our able colleagues in the MFA, most notably, Randy Bates (primarily a nonfiction writer but also an award-winning poet), and in the English department by Earle Bryant, Nancy Easterlin, Carolyn Hembree, Niyi Osundare, Doreen Piano, Peter Schock, Les White, and others – as well as by poets working exclusively for the Low Residency MFA – Bill Lavender, Shelley Puhak, Susan Schultz, Peter Thompson, and others. Probably our leanest moment occurred in the fall of 2006 when only one new student poet, Kari Shisler, matriculated. But the intrepid Shisler brought with her an unflagging spirit, resourceful character, and worldly sensibility that was enough to compensate for any five new students, and in the following years she found herself in the company of a new dynamic generation of poets! Poets were not alone among the creative writers in working for recovery and survival, both professionally and personally, post-Katrina, during Jindal's administration; with Knudsen's loss, the MFA and Low Residency MFA engaged several writers on a temporary basis – successful alumni Joseph Boyden, Amanda Boyden, and Barb Johnson in fiction writing, Patrice Melnick in nonfiction writing, and Eric Overmeyer and Henry Griffin in screenwriting. And students kept applying and enrolling.

In truth, though, regardless of New Orleans's popular reputation for being "the city that care forgot" and a city where at any given moment you can find a street parade in one neighborhood, a gala crawfish party in another, and a spontaneous jazz session in a club in another, austerity more than any other condition over the years seems to have tethered the city's most important public university like a jess on a falcon. Still, largely due to the untold energy, imagination, and drive of more than a generation of graduate students by now who have arrived from all over the U.S. and elsewhere, the MFA program continues to soar. In addition to the annual poetry awards, other prizes, and special events sponsored by the MFA, students inevitably spawn their own reading series, publications, special opportunities, and collaborative projects – often through their association with *Bayou* and through meeting UNO MFA alumni who have taken up more or less permanent residence in the city. Although it has had a variety of names over the years, each year a popular monthly reading series is organized, publicized, and well attended by MFA students; the most sustained name has been The Gold Room series, carrying forward the name of a UNO series originally staged in the "Gold Room" of what had been the Scottish Rite Masonic Temple built in 1920 on St. Charles Avenue in downtown New Orleans. The room was designed more like a courtroom or nave in a cathedral than an auditorium, with hard wooden pews at right angles facing a raised bench and a vaulted ceiling; to read there, a poet might feel the need either to preach a sermon, publicly confess her or his sins, or plead not to be sent to the dungeons below (which must have been there). Yet the room brought out the best humor and writing of those who read their work. Currently, the series thrives at the more congenial and lively Pelican Bay restaurant on Elysian Fields Avenue, owned and operated by novelist and UNO alumnus Maurice Ruffin.

My estimate is that in that fifteen-year stretch before and after Katrina, despite a very lean budget for graduate fellowships and assistantships, as well as increased demands put on faculty because of the losses to retirement and other jobs, Murphy, our Instructor colleague Carolyn Hembree, and I taught, mentored, and directed more than sixty poets toward completing their degrees. In all its genres, the MFA program year after year consistently leads the university in both the number of advanced degrees awarded and in the completion rate at the graduate level. Eventually, through the mysterious workings by Rick Barton on the eve of his own retirement as Creative Writing Director and full-time faculty, in 2012 the MFA program experienced a renaissance in welcoming a new generation of faculty members virtually in one fell swoop: fiction writers Barb Johnson and Neal Walsh, playwright Justin Maxwell, nonfiction writer Richard Goodman, and poet Carolyn Hembree. To be sure, in poetry, Hembree as an Instructor at UNO since 2001 had already drawn attention to herself through her teaching poetry writing classes at all levels, her tireless mentoring of students, her securing of funds for visiting poets from Poets & Writers and other outside sources, and her drawing serious attention to her own work from editors and granting agencies. With her background in both academia and intensive training in drama, to go with her literary studies at Birmingham-Southern College and the University of Arizona MFA program, Hembree has a penchant for adopting voices both on paper and in her classroom that can electrify students, waking them up to wide possibilities for poetry they hadn't dreamed of. Her own work can cause the plaster in the room to crack, and her pedagogy leaves no room for the timid to remain comfortably quiet, yet she inspires confidence and, uniquely among poets, a strange loyalty from her students. Together with her new creative writing colleagues, Hembree has injected the MFA program with a twenty-first century serum stirring up not only a new generation of poets and writers, who are already publishing widely in print and on the internet, garnering a record number of Pushcart nominations, and publishing chapbooks and new collections throughout the U.S., but invigorating in them the same catholicity in technique, style, range, and voices that has guided both the instruction in and the production of poetry by graduate students at UNO since its inception. While poets at UNO may not expect to find easy enthusiasm or acceptance for their individual poems inside or outside class – and while most of them at one point or another find themselves in crisis, whether a crisis of confidence, crisis of voice, or crisis of purpose, in immersing themselves in this most solitary of the arts – what they do discover (among other students as well as faculty) are genuine readers of their work, readers unfazed by current literary fashion or social prejudice, readers ready to measure and weigh their poems, phrase by phrase, strophe by strophe, image by image, trope by trope. Any poet unable to cherish such readers might well look right through the UNO MFA program and carry on famously, but the true character of the UNO poetry program, I think, dwells in this communal aspect of its labor, day after day, year after year.

Through its first quarter century (the second quarter century of UNO itself), the MFA program in Creative Writing has steadily developed a reputation for itself – mostly off the map, of course, in comparison to the well-endowed, highly acclaimed, or otherwise sexy creative writing graduate programs throughout the U.S. – of being an off-center sanctuary for serious writers of every stripe (indeed, including those in prison stripes, from time to time). Here writers matriculate to plunge themselves into their own reading and exploring their writing potential, often emerging by having to admit to themselves, almost begrudgingly, that they actually did learn a lot about writing and reading during their degree program, not only from their instructors but from their peers, their newly discovered, now lifelong collaborators and literary co-conspirators, whether in poetry, fiction, nonfiction, playwriting, or screenwriting. By reputation, poets, mostly, unlike prose writers, tend to remain standoffish, highly suspicious of other writers, especially other poets. Or maybe I am only speaking of myself when I say that. But what I do often observe, in general, is that the last thing a poet wants is for her or his own voice to sound too much like some other poet's voice, whether it be Edna St. Vincent Millay's, Amiri Baraka's, Bob Hicok's, or that classmate's across the seminar room. Not at all! I want to be merely yet entirely original; otherwise, I may as well quit this calling altogether. Yet strangely, after the experience more than once of an intense fourteen weeks in a creative writing class, full of butting heads, scratching elbows, whispering rumors, and kicking shins under the table with a cadre of minds unlike myself, a bizarre kinship can grow inside. And a keen poet can end up feeling artistically, even spiritually, intimate with other poets, not despite but because of their stylistic and visionary disparities. Their very differences (which seem to differ differently each year), their sensibilities seemingly as disconnected in technique and subject matter as they are collaborative in energy and effort, end up enjoining UNO poets, not as a "school" but as a brood of poets, as much attached as birds hatched in a common nest, or maybe as a laity, as those in a congregation who may share nothing but their mutual faith in this finally unknown, immeasurable art. This is the kinship, I think, that will be evident to any close reader of the poems in this anthology.

Visiting Poets at The Creative Writing Workshop and
the Low-Res Program
1980-2018

Ralph Angel

Maya Angelou

John Ashbery

Eric Baus

Elana Bell

Jorge Luis Borges

Darrell Bourque

Jericho Brown (UNO MFA 2002)

Paula Closson Buck

Megan Burns

Marilyn Chin

Chanel Clarke

Peter Cooley

Philip Dacey

Tom Dent

Toi Derricotte

Ed Dorn

Sebastien Doubinsky

Michael Tod Edgerton

Gina Ferrara (UNO MFA 2008)

Annie Finch

Lucia Getsi

Dana Gioia

Elton Glaser (UNO BA 1966?/MA 1968?)

Lara Glenum

R.S. Gwynn
Marilyn Hacker
Derreck Harriell
Kelly Harris
Robert Hass
Ava Leavell Haymon
Cynthia Hogue
Jay Hopler
Allison Joseph
Donald Justice
Julie Kane
Yusef Komunyakaa
Hank Lazer
Denise Levertov
Everette Maddox
Bernadette Mayer
Shara McCallum
Jeredith Merrin
Laura Mullen
David Mura
Biljana Obradovic
Brenda Marie Osbey
Wang Ping
Shelley Puhak (Low Res UNO MFA 2004)
Ishmael Reed
Trisha Rezende (UNO MFA 2008)
Adrienne Rich
Brad Richard
Sheryl St. Germain

Mona Lisa Saloy

Metta Sama

Ed Sanders

Jean-Mark Sens

Martha Serpas

Chris Shipman

Richard Siken

Dave Smith

John Warner Smith (Low Res UNO MFA 2012)

William Jay Smith

Katherine Soniat

Lorenzo Thomas

Rodrigo Toscano

Eric Tretheway (UNO MA 1974?)

Frederick Turner

Ellen Bryant Voigt

Patricia A.Ward (UNO MFA 1998)

Afton Wilky

Laurie A. Williams (UNO MFA 2009)

Miller Williams

Jake Adam York

Al Young

Andy Young

On a Wednesday Night

Carolyn Hembree

On a Wednesday night in spring, poets gathered around a table in a university classroom on a former military base in New Orleans. Having exchanged pages and whispered lines to one another for more than an hour, our conference table's tempered glass top spontaneously exploded. As we later learned, members of the workshop convening downstairs heard the deafening boom and believed some terrific event had occurred above their heads. Yet, they neither evacuated nor came to our aid, understanding the location of true emergency: the poem in front of them. In fact, all rock-ribbed poets of the CWW persisted that night with my class brushing off shards to continue our weekly meeting. If the habits of poets might be likened to those of the cat or the ox, an analogy made by Susan Wood, then an abundance of oxen populate the University of New Orleans Creative Writing Workshop.

In 2012, I joined the CWW as an assistant professor and took up my yoke. For ten years prior to my professorship, I was a UNO instructor who served on thesis committees and attended visiting poet events, MFA proms, annual banquets, and graduate readings. The culture of our program, a culture characterized by authenticity, rigor, and generosity, was established decades prior to my promotion. Cellist Gary Hoffman's words to a young musician capture my experience of joining this community: "'You're coming into the middle of the thing. The music's been going on all the time. You're just now hearing it, picking it up, letting it come through you.'"[1]

Being an insider in the program has increased my admiration for CWW candidates, alumni, and faculty. Presented with university cutbacks and natural disasters, their tenacity has been proven too many times. Trusting bonds formed during periods of relative calm must sustain them. At the beginning of the academic year, returning students welcome new students through potluck

---

1 Marianne Boruch, *In the Blue Pharmacy*. (San Antonio: Trinity University, 2005) p. 180.

meals and Parkview gatherings. From what I have observed, these rituals—none of them formalized—contribute to a cultural legacy passed from one class to the next. Visiting writers to our program comment on the supportive atmosphere of our workshops and the aesthetic diversity of student poems.

"But somewhere along the line, from my heroes, whose souls were forged in fires infinitely hotter than mine, I gained an outsized faith in articulation itself as its own form of protection," writes Maggie Nelson in her hybrid memoir *The Argonauts*. Flannery O'Connor proffered that creative writing teachers are useful insomuch as we suggest helpful reading material. With these assertions in mind, I require each workshop member to study a "mentor" poet for a semester in hopes that she will continue to seek mentorship through books after the program has ended.

For an end-of-semester reading, I composed a cento inspired by my students and their mentor poets. The cento, Latin for "cloak made of patches," originated in the third or fourth century and is comprised of lines from other poems. A cento is never *mine* but *ours*. The rules are as follows: two lines from the same source may not appear back-to-back, and lines must be reproduced in their entirety or halved with both hemistichs included in the cento. "CENTO 6163-601" includes two lines from each student in my Fall 2014 workshop and one line from each mentor poet.[2] You will likely be able to identify the mentors (hint: open with Lorde, close with Dante). I present our cento as one recent artifact from my steadfast community, the Creative Writing Workshop.

February 3, 2018

2 My workshop section included the following students: Joe Buckley, Jessica Morey-Collins, Tyler Gillespie, Kia Groom, Wren Hanks, Clare Harmon, Jade Hurter, Laurin DeChae, Nate Kostar, and Spencer Silverthorne.

CENTO 6163-601

for and of my students

Take my word for jewel in your open light
inferno: I fall from my mouth by thousands
through riptide of rhythms and the metaphor's seaweed
and through the conversational spaces, after,
for the risk John! For the risk itself! It's exhilarating!

Held in the globes of
thrash and torment, angelic harpy music,
this too is history—
what speaks in a stolen voice
they tossed at the stage.
(The boys think so at least.)

Error 404 not found refresh repeat error.
I do not wish to speak to your machine.

Call me by my first name—
O shit it's already been published.
(No second coming when I'm gone).

This is for the shitkickers in the world who know how much liquid
eyeliner it takes:
do not hate the sterile scentless crepe myrtle.

Just snakes
are my perfect mouthpiece,
singing each new leaf out of each tree
and binding with briars, my joys & desires.

They do not talk.
They speak to you in museum manifestations.
They're waiting to be murdered.

Inscribed by [Redacted] bearing ghost marks of [Redacted],
the words won't change again.
Throbbing amoeba, torn from nothing,
sad friend, you cannot change.

From well rested soils,
specifically that fire
where I can go to visit with my ancestors,
I climbed out, tired of waiting.

The garment took on an explosive sheen.
I found myself within a forest dark.

GRADUATE POEMS

Reports from the Laser Interferometer Gravitational-Wave Observatory

Nordette N. Adams

Two black holes
colliding—the LIGO chirp—
echo of celestial bodies bump-
ing a billion years ago.   Brief spark.
"More energy than all the stars conjoined."

The ripple turned
            into the rising of greater masses
                  merging.
The chirp's interpolated so
the universe speaks a swoosh of odd sucks
and swallows when spacetime curves under gravitational flow.
Over us, these waves wash, unseen.   We are senseless.
            We feel nothing
while the universe works hard, works,
                       drawing in its blown-up bits.
            Does it model love?

When the wormhole finally forms, we can slip
arms through ether like Mr. Spock, we are told,
and touch moments of mistakes made.
Will we seek the second we fell off-track
and squish between our fingers the white,
brown, yellow, black fences men constructed?

"The universe has rhythm. Listen."

We listen and we listen.
  We are small,
            must collect our blown-up bits,
seek the universal beat till we sway
as one great body.
When we sway as one great body,
we will *swoosh*.

Sidebar While Making a Bucket List

Nordette N. Adams

. . . and write more about nothing. Seize
lily privilege.
                    Black poets
deserve that luxury, writing about nothing—
sometimes—to speak for no one—
rest their backs on deep lush green and gaze up
at blue and fluffy.

Let us exhale and give no account for
every black person in this shaded world,
every black mug shot on the 6:00 news,
every black politician with Jack Horner thumbs high, and
every black bit of fleshiness:
        girls' short-shorts hiked on brown-bubble cheeks,
        boys' pants, beltless, flaunting cracks of brown asses.
How loud the black mass is.
How single the black mother.
How absent the black daddy.
How high the black jobless.
How low the black test scores.
How natural the black athlete.
How well fare the black folk.

"Tell us how we, whites, can do anything better."
"Explain yourself, Great, mythic black monolith."
"And just what does Kendrick Lamar mean?"

    No.

For a little while, just cuddly light letters, no sharp
leaden syllables pressing down shoulders.
No ashes and sackcloth. Thorny diadem, off!

. . . and write a poem about my love, a red red rose, pen
an ode on urns, a stanza on fans of budding twigs, a naughty flea.

When will we ever at leisure paper the world
with navel meditations then recline on the plush
green mountain and dine by the brook dreaming
our raisins in rain not sun.

Eldora Whitley's Quilt

Mawiyah Kai EL-Jamah Bomani

This poem was created after viewing the photograph of Jennine Pettway and another girl with the quilter Jorena Pettway in 1937, Arthur Rothstein is the photographer.

Listen whilst I quilt little darlings
hold tightly the threshold of your story
this here a tale that is every bit African
as it is Black American   read what the swatches say
don't care nothing what white folks say
we didn't ask to come here to Indian territory
and Indians didn't ask for no white man
                              to run them way from the land of their gods
then turn round and label them as
                              Indian givers
steada white folks calling themselves   white man stealers
read the swatches   not them history books   fulla untruths
manner of speaking girls
this patch here tells the story
of how we was carted over salty water
stacked head to foot
sometimes bosom to bosom
floating in feces and other folks urine
we was sardines in a wooden can   a carpet of wall to wall flesh
times was hard then as they is now
that boat ride was the negro holocaust
that's why   here girls   right here in this patch
                                        the stars is fulla blood
few folks get that reference
                    what they see is stars crying
every time I pull out this quilt to cover mrs. mable on the deaconess board
or elder johnson the father of St. John the Baptist Tabernacle
they ask *how come the sky is fulla blood sister eldora*
and girls I tell them that's cause the eguns them African ancestors
living in the sky done cried all the water from they eye sockets

got nothing left but blood covered pupils
first thing they bloody tears hit   is stars
people who knows what folks live beyond the stars understand
those who don't   assume the stars is crying
better yet   armageddon's on the horizon   but not in my quilt
the eguns are crying tears of blood
and see this patch it's the after effect
        of bloody tears soaking into the earth
what you see growing are Sankofa birds
I got hundreds of them gracing this quilt
read what they say   you all book smart
they say *cut your chains and you is free*
cut your roots and you is as good as dead
somewhere along the course of your life
girls you gon see fit to understand
this quilt got more sense
than them school books you all be reading
this patch tells the beginning of you alls
great great great uncle moonwalker
he was an Indian man with specks of tan
so that made him part Black part Indian
but he could do a good job of passing for either
he got the name moonwalker cause he was harriet tubman
before she was herself
why he freed a plenty enslaved Africans
with animal hearing and a bow an arrow   draped cross-ways his back
truth is the light   cause I don't deal in fairytales
black folks ain't got no patience to be once upon a timing
we need to live in the real world   with our eyes wide open
somewhere along the course of your life
            that one gon slap you in the face too
                        just you wait and see
anyhow moonwalker rescued your aunt makeda
and this scrap is from her and his wedding day clothes
the two pieces of fabric was joined together
just like they was   African and Indian blood
whoa lawd a powerful mixture
mixture of ain't gon be none cause we ain't gon take none

feel this whole row   where the dogs is running and the stream passes
  from dusk to dawn
this big house is master charlie matthew's plantation in lafayette looseiana
where moonwalker snatched his bride
and ole charlie lost a lot of his cotton pickers and cane breakers
                                        to the masterful mind of moonwalker
oh girls I could go on and on about this section of patches
and the lynching of my mama's brother jeremiah
for smacking the daylights out of a white man
who called his mama a picky headed nigger bitch
lawd jesus girls
I could spend all day in this here row of killing fields
lynchings mutilated black men and boys
they took trinkets of flesh from jeremiah's backside
                                  and sewed them into wallets
I knows that to be the truth
cause my mama don't fancy lies
just as much as I have a distaste for fairy tales
this here patch is the sheriff at that time riding his horse
waving the wallet made from jeremiah's backside
in the air as the whistle of his fire-stick brightens
the night sky into a burst of orange
girls girls girls
these times we living in ain't much better
I thought this patch here   us migrating to the north
would bring us better days   happy days
                              many less crying eguns
but right in front you   you got several patches of white folks angry
                                at negroes
they believe was stealing they jobs right from under they American flag
fulla stars stripes and white folks rights ONLY
see this   this patch is for your daddy's brother luke
stabbed forty-four times   just cause he had the audacity
to ask for the same rights as white workers
men he had worked side by side at that factory with
men who had eaten his wife's sweet potato pie
licked every morsel from their fingers these same band of brothers
had summoned enough anger and hate to take him way from this world

all these patches here and there
are every apartment we ever lived in and got taken from us
cause white folks needed a residence in a time of soup kitchens and
  desperation
the pieces I'm working on now girls is us coming from
mills general store just a few weeks ago
and finding the doors locked and here you two is looking
peering through the window (as folks say)
witnessing a blonde girl in between both you in age
sleeping in the bed you two shared together
see why fairytales don't sit right with me
cause they fulla vengeance at times and
  at others fulla stuff that's undeserving to they characters
characters who just trying to make due make it through
with the hand god give em goldilox sleeping in yo bed
is a lot less cute when the bears ain't got no choice but to evict themselves
cause bears ain't got rights just like us
bears is un-American less they grow up knowing how
to vote for the right cause the white cause
I'm bout tired of quilting for today girls
lets go clean some mustards
it's a good day for mustards
lets go little darlings
yo history ain't going no where
it'll be here time we finish eating eager to be embraced
by an old woman's soothing
yet calloused
caress

The Black Angel

Jonathan Brown

I have a black angel fish I've been trying to figure out how to discipline.
She nips at the other fishes' fins. Seems to be nothing I can do about it.

I could starve her but then I'd harm the other fish.
Isn't that always the way? You paying for someone else's sins?

As if morality had a balance or swimming
in your own piss wasn't enough already?

You know that part in your favorite song where everything crescendos
and you head bang in your kitchen when no one else is around?

Maybe that part sticks in the black angel's head and she only want
to be alone. Or maybe the other fish don't know

they're in a mosh pit. No matter. It's all forgotten
as soon as I walk away. I'm no fish boss.

Sure, I have to change the water. Sure, I have to feed them,
watch them, and ask them questions. I can't

blame them for not answering. They can't talk
yet, but I'm teaching them to read by stacking *Time*

magazines against the back of the glass. I watch and wait
for the sake of the others. Hopefully, reading will teach them love or patience.

Permanently in Medias Res

Jonathan Brown

Lately I wake up outside
my body hovering
        roughly six feet
above my bed, but sometimes

        I'm under the bed.
One time I got stuck in the trunk of my car. Couldn't
escape that one until I woke up.
        Watching my self sleep
from the perspective
        of the ceiling fan

really used to creep me out
and still does,
especially when I see
        the hand
reaching towards
my face but can't
        tell whose hand
or whose face.

        If you withdraw
from the skin
and everything in it,
will the residue
of time
        be left
behind?

        A minute-sized-dent?
        Perhaps an hour
scattered throughout the suitcases
        cartooned in place
for the sake of verisimilitude.
        After all, we're traveling, right?

When in a disembodied point of view
do you take everything with you?

No matter. Now I have to put myself together
for the rest
of the day. However,
there's no
way I can do that if a third of my better faculties blur
or refuse
to mingle between the woke and the dream state.

I need to find my kneecaps,
and as soon as I do,
I'm headed to the coffee maker.
Is there anything you
need me to bring back?

Is nothing all
or nothing?

In Other News

Joseph Buckley

Larger than the width of the sidewalk,
    larger than cars: yes, larger

than the boy bundled to his eyes in wool.
    The tail was purple, the tail

was green-spotted, the tail connected
    to a Tyrannosaurus-Rex,

who curled under newspaper blankets,
    headlines reading: *Snow*.

Snow covered the dinosaur. Snow fell
    over buildings, signs, and eyes

for years. As far back as anyone could recall: snow.
    Villainous-insistence, relentless insistently

the white came. Dreamy white powder,
    permeable white, moldable

as bars of soap; Over the beast's dead-gray skin,
    the boy laid his scarf.

Sparring with Words

Joseph Buckley

Day and night he sat
at a desk built to conjure

from the depths, of space,
from branches in his window

framed by the light holding
bright birds who sang

to him poems, as he typed,
My love is like…

Papers crumpled and piled
around him. Each typewriter

clack consumed more
of the man's strength.

Misfired attempts surrounded
him like so many opponents,

horrified and subsumed by black
letters like cataracts in his eyes.

He blindly punched the keys
until they slapped their beauty

onto the white.

Conversations at Night

Joseph Buckley

A pane of glass divides a mannequin
from the raindrops that punctuate my skin.
I lean close to the glass to touch
the heat of its never-night world:

The heat of the flat beach scene
the mannequin poses by with a hand
in the come hither position. I tell
the mannequin the names of my children, pets, and wife.
I tell how I can't keep any of my houseplants
alive and my lack of faith in having faith.
I try to communicate my inability
to distinguish between a lover and barbed wire,
between surfeit and shame.
I try to tell a joke.

My breath leaves a bloom of fog on the window
and my face leaves three holes in the bloom.
I ask the mannequin if it knows
a place with good margaritas
and could I join it in its life
on the other side of the window.
Next to the picture of white sand,
green trees and a cruise ship,
all the tiny people wave themselves off
to a place, I so clearly dream.

Symmetry of a Purge

Lauren Capone

I've lost my head again, forgive.
Half the time it's poison I mop up

Scarring like glaciers
Dredged through a canal

Of muck and sand. I still think I am
The rise of sun to one.

Of fish, its stillness coats my pores.
In decay, paint. Catch the light and I blush.

If it is symmetry, (one I can't break),
Tomorrow will bring potted Paperwhites—

Mouths agape, as though telling.
Tell me—

A red wool sweater, bleeding pomegranates,
Brass rings encrypted with a truth:

Is it the small ones who purge themselves the most,
Pinned in a rough of rust and spent coffee?

Conflagration
And the stuff that enters a soul.

Stuff it with cotton through the mouth.
An empty taxidermy and small.

My cheek pressed against the wet body.

Study in Perspective on South Beach

Lauren Capone

Winds break waves blue-white crashing. No, aqua, a translucent aqua, like cellophane. The sea made of cellophane. Hanging over the horizon, the sun: everything flat. Sun-bathers, boats, planes grow smaller as they leave me. Let's take the boat on the edge, two more boats today than yesterday. They are just as small. Heavy boots worn by men working on the boat, even smaller, I'm thinking the size of my pinky fingernail. I'm thinking of their skin, leathered. Their hands, calloused. Their shirts, thin cotton. What are they doing out there? Fishing? It can't be rigging—there are too many people swimming. I tell myself they are looking after the waters even though I know it isn't true. I know the boats are heavy as war ships, but from here they don't look that way. One day when I looked at the boat, it looked like a prisoner in isolation. Yes. Yes, they are looking after the waters. Mixing the perfect blue, sending the waves to shore. Not men, no. These are women on this boat. What was I thinking? These women staring into the sun flat sun. The huge thing, the boat, is it on her back? These shells, this sand, these are her jewels. The waves, her billowy pants.

transcendental ethel

Carrie Chappell

6. *once,*

i// was a girl
scout.

to this day,

i// can be
long-winded
on the subject
of canoes, camp-
fire songs, rope,
kindling. listen,

5. i// want to go away.

/
/

another breath, another bemoan—love
is an always crisis.   corn was never my credo,
so i// never went wishing for someone there.

you know where. i// cut a rug and ran into a
tapisserie. there joined the campaign, the
circus. i// mean, i//
began caring, became

careful-

minded. a careless. fucking joy-lover. joy-

digger. oh joy. ode.   odious.   oedipus.   i // think we are
    blind, that the directions to our best

regions are lost in our eyes. joy. is held in a sweaty
palm or in a green field of (ode to) soy. don't listen. don't look

for someone. for somewhere there. don't go looking for it.
i// swear. it's better to get lost on the little stuff.
to take the helm
of a candy bar. like. take me for instance,

a girl
scout
at heart, wanting, what (?)
only a cookie
and to use my

skills.

4. from what i// remember, i// do know, do now

—bees do run
from snapping
fingers, snakes
from ground-
stomping, and kindness

above all, humility, too.—

yesterday,

you pointed me
down a trail. *gosh,*

thank you,

/
/

3. for pointing the way

to the future—

an american girl has options. a girl scout no less. has options, is
what they'll say.

and the dreams will ignite. and for some paris. for paris some
will ignite.

how to live it:

version 1: be a woman's woman, but live for men, love the ones you're with but also the far-aways. spend your time. telling everybody you miss them and then eat your blues in baguettes. own jewelry but wish to accept more, be bi-lingual curious! be baby-sitter swank! stomp the ground for snakes. wait for scooters, the kiss, the la defense legs, be ok with champagne pictures until. until.
*(*dream referred*
to on most paris blogs.)

/
/

*version 2: be a poet, ok, maybe just a writer, hang yourself up on homonyms, find yourself often taken with simple French rhymes: dommage chômage! dommage fromage!, be happy being cute for French men for a week until feminist moods set in, then find a new one, snap your fingers at the proverbial bees, be a functioning drunk, functioning introvert, try to break the stereotype.(*dream deferred, citation:*
too difficult.)

/
/

i// think that's it.

2. *so, they shut me up in booze—and*

i// am, i// professed, a troubled
roamantic—i// fit your—i//am *the*
daguerreotyped. as when a little
girl moves to a dream place,
calling yesterdays into—*like*

everybody i// sat upon a table, eating
mixed meats. everyone stood in my
way. and i// felt a friendly nothing. i //

had my tools—a set of earrings
succinctly wed to my lobes, a pair
of pants that blacked with every black,
and *a* you, distant person somehow
made into the criminal so i// could stand

myself,
away, spewing forth my *jesus christs*
just enough to make a small religion,
just enough to cast iron the long
breath of my short history. *go. go forth, for christ's sake forward,* i// said

to myself, *hither filth, fortune.*

1. there, here—

with my planets arestin' and my
chambers full of speech, i// lie
still in the thought of my many
shelters.   i// have fallen

where i// fall

and wandered out, a girl pulling
at her wet shorts tight and
knotting at the crotch. being
stranded wasn't near as bad as
i// had thought, i// had lived and

tamed a many a thing. glares
more genuine exhausted in
their ravines, where trees
stand like old men, lampposts   poles to be
vaulted and i // a girl

scout sashaying where
bees grip
my ankles, picking with honey
spines the flesh i// i// i//   storm(ed) in.

I. New Place, Stratford, April 1615

Barbara Darcey

The light of morning replaces
syllables of grief, dust dancing in the red veins
and the taste of butterscotch remaining
from the dram of whisky consumed to obliviate
the face of my beloved

The heroes are the first to dissolve
like salt in a carafe stirred and stirred
to soothe the savage throat

Hamnet was eleven when he left us
Strafing our heart with the sounds, defunct now,
of his voice calling across the lawns of Warwickshire
to Judith

My stance has been to leave the weeping to Ann
and I crossed the land to London
and made our name a veritable army of sound
fury desire and death. Death above us always
in the catwalks of Blackfriars

And beneath awaits like the second best bed, which
in case she was wondering, is the grave. And grave I am
as I await the end pursued by the stage directions.
Exeunt. I realized after a fashion that it all ends and mortality
is our reward, even at eleven, even at fifty-one, and always

So go I there. Perhaps one evening next year. I will embrace
my son

II. 17 Feet Down, Warwickshire 1616

Barbara Darcey

and curst be he that moves my bones

The thought has occurred to me before
I have entombed my fate
and borne the curse of triumph *ad infinitum*

Upon my casket shall lay one thousand
roses, each a moment remembered
and hereby interred

Remember your brother, my girl,
even as you take your man against
your father's will

Remember the final escape of us all
is the same, the plot persists among
the equivalencies and the different trade routes

I have mapped the globe in my way
and tore off the pages, a folio incomplete
as the short life of your twin

The evasion of plague was illusory
for life's the plague and our houses
are pocked with it. Sooner or later

It comes down to the chalice, the vicar
the prayer behind the curtain
final notices in the playhouse closed

until further notice
by order of the new King

The Unburning Heart of Percy Bysshe

Barbara Darcey

for Mary

Locked in your chest
is a steak-red
source, a pump:
In the center
is a torn page
from your life

It is the final page
of an epic
perhaps about a creator
and a creature

So the heart banks
sharply left, avoids
the precipice
while the hand writes
The Cenci

True tales of daring
and tragedy:
children lost
and a wife gazing
into the depths
of a fragile glass jar

The Age of Stuttering

James Thurston Davis

Sucking in was like reaching a hilltop.
The smoke spiked the lungs, ripped
out the throat, star-speckled
the eyes & tongued the brain.
I could see the back of my teeth,
taste earwax. The purple plastic tube
belched like a fire-breathing dragon
as Weaver's Camaro snaked the lakefront
curves, a metallic reptile waddling
in time to "Rock Candy," the day
scaled back to headache. My mom
was the only child of a hawk
& pounced on my red-caked eyes
straight off. In every dream I'm reeling
from some girl who moved away,
a dog that died in a fight, pear
smear on the sidewalk, blue bike
stolen from the yard. After she busted me,
I filled my lines with rattle wheels,
marooned on my blind mind beach.
Dialed into the Age of Stuttering
& strapped into my tight slacks,
I often let the scent drive the car,
my numb lips slurring to the end.

Lame by Then

James Thurston Davis

Driving all night across featureless Texas
we passed La Grange as shadows
appeared behind a stand of cypress.
I'd given up cigarettes, couldn't sleep
anyway, so we just went straight
through to Austin. In the hotel
highrise, I couldn't tell west from east,
the morning sun wakening the evening
traffic, bedspreads shrouding
all the way to the floor from the ceiling,
and we stomped our road-fed
jet jag with orange juice,
stale doughnuts branded in gothic font.
Somehow I'm thrust into seminars
on the music of business, the vitality
of ties, the suspension of distortion
and disbelief in legal contracts,
staring at the perfumed faces,
my grimy neon shoelaces no longer hip,
just sad. You were late, and I didn't know
Austin had an airport until I picked you up
that night, by then the twenty-sixth
hour of my day. Already diagnosed
and camouflaged on lithium, you pushed
my camera away, left me standing in the lot.
The gig was lame by then, the trip
the anticlimax of the decade. No one
remembered your movie role
overshadowed by killer bees and broken beads.
Mouth stuffed with flowers, you couldn't sing
if you wanted to, and home as far away
as October, when you walked into your room
and never came out.

the sensorium of the cyborg

Laurin DeChae

power on: i a homegrown miracle,
a lovething made for amber lighting
and divine in all the wrong spaces.
but i feeling galactic, a moon-eyed honey-
soaked blip on a screen in a world egg-like and lilting.
i orients herself but without the perception
of time, walks newborn deer-like,
tongues a grape skin, a blueberry flesh,
a pebble, a diamond. i has a mouth
of gold and a voice of static and no one
to understand her when she mutters.
i tastes like midnight when she tests
the wind with her finger. tastes flight
then part of i is grounded and part
floats in the ether with the bodies
who have lost their names. i dares not
call them specters, rather stars
set on fire. i wanted to lose her name, but
i a fool on a journey, a glittermeat dreamboat.
i thinks, *my skin peels back and makes i pretty*
soft, pretty prismatic, pretty little thing.
i throws a temper tantrum
because i gets what i wants.
i just wants to feel magical
without having to be magical.
silver-skinned-eve-come-lightly,
her system fractures dramatic
so i doesn't watch black and white films
because i thinks they lack depth.
instead i makes her own scenes, makes
sense of her own otherworldly,
i, with nothing but a flowersack
to keep her warm. i a burlap dress
come into sensation interrupted.

where there is _______ i sees _______ .
now you see her, now, now,
i doesn't want to be here.
i doesn't want to be i
but i was made to machine,
made to sluice her shedding
snakeskin, she capsule and container.
what i knows as truth or prophecy:
i mirror distortion dysmorphia—
big head, little ankles.
i's insides feel like coral reefs,
i tickled pink, but i's skin
church hymns crows sing.
i is dazzled by the bright lights
of big cities but her body is so quiet,
so hush, that is, overlapped.
i always floats and never touches
because to touch means to stay a while.
i has layers: dry wind and damp swells.
the roof of i's mouth is mountains,
her throat a wheezebox, insides chromatic
pulp. she knows nothing of herself so she bites
her tongue and bleeds, compares herself to seashells
and the scent of beige, a freshly fired gun—
skinmetal or fleshflower—that one summer
her trashjewels sang of high heels and hoofprints
and she's been hungry and throbbing ever since.

THE SPECTACLE OF THE HYBRID

an ars poetica

Laurin DeChae

> *If a painter should wish to unite a horse's neck to a human head, and spread a variety of plumage over limbs [of different animals] taken from every part [of nature], so that what is a beautiful woman in the upper part terminates unsightly in an ugly fish below; could you, my friends, refrain from laughter, were you admitted to such a sight.*
>
> —Horace, "Ars Poetica"

1. the speaker speaks on her experience with a glittering mouthpiece

[CLOSE ON the stiff curio, exhibit plaque—
the only gold she wears.]
she misses the chain with her name
coiled in cursive—astrid.
her hand is there,
at her throat forever
pointing to herself.
she is afraid of her own name,
but i promises she
is user friendly
because mathematically
subject + object = pleasure.
here she tessellates
killing the lights.
what to do with me

2. where is i located in spacetime that she floats so ambiguously?

in her glass casing
amorphous simulacra
or animalia amalgam?
pinned under specimen

viewing glass, she
breathes moss/eats paper.
she is that which she created,
an i sick with body poems
with permission to touch
the world diagonally

Outthere where they said
your hair is so _________
your waist is so _________
your skin.

what makes me unmakes me.
if my eyes were clocks
and my ears telephones,
my motherwounds,
throbbing,
could burst.

3. how coded the body politic that they may ask "what are you"?

variously known as: halfies, halfbreeds, mutts
two different *species*   conjoined in   fractions or fractals
i as experiment
i as subject   removed & replaced   contiguous still
beast/creature/meat   cycles of hatching
spawning & sporing

toni morrison's grandmother said
she could tell by the shade
of her granddaughter's skin
that she had been tampered with.
that's what we used to say, she said
what makes me unmakes me, i says.

i straps a beak to her face,
to her leg, a fin. affixes
a wire to her tongue

strings to her limbs,
a humming mutation.
what are you?

look at her trying to speak   in stars.
instead she writes scripts for her dolls
with titles like "mannequin kisses the mirror
as if she's catching the last train" and
"mannequin and dummy make love
on the washing machine."
what a cliché

4. *how does the manuscript examine themes of double consciousness?*

her lover tells her she can't grow plants
which is to say
her seat belt arm holds her in.
i holds space
which is basically
holding air
which is basically
holding
nothing
and everything.

i wants to talk to whoever
writes in the margins:
tensions btwn violence & survival,
wants to write in the margins
herself, but who is she
to take up all that space?

she, made of fruit, made of scales,
her body flickering
in the *raza cosmica,*
her puppet mouthhole
froze open.
they are trying to make her talk,

to parrot a part
the world from the world,
a dream-making machine,
slick with honey and buzzing.

i got what i deserves

Laurin DeChae

all i wants is song lyrics for breakfast
and to come thickly at lunch. i could give
or take dinner/ in form of candlelight
or in absolutes served cold. can i get
a witness to her hunger? all this
steel moonlight can make an i starsick
with fever. a spoonful of sugar with her
medicine because i can be so childish.
where else to project all this longing?
i waits for skies to speak, thinks
tell me what to say and i'll say it,
pours herself a drink. another spoonfool.
i fumbles while dressing, puts an arm
where a head should be. goes with it.
quacks her hand puppet-like. waits
to see if anyone will notice
her haircut. i does herself up.
all this jewelry and nowhere to go
all this makeup and no face to show.
i doesn't believe in god but believes
that someone is keeping her alive
for magic tricks and spawns. knows life
as hands not hers. i banks on breaking
the carousel whose faded song mocks her
like all songs do. the world turns and we
away from ourselves headlong and furious.
pulling her hair to the side and turning i
asks *get my zipper? peel i apart at the seam?*

Dear

Aurielle Destiche

While eating starlight for breakfast, she writes me a letter. Her tongue can no longer form syllables, but her hands make origami from bellflowers after wringing the petals for ink. She tells me she folds lines into my hair at night to help me remember them in the morning

clementines drop to the bed / we pull up the morning sky to block out the sun

She tells me my prayers taste heavy and salty, but she puts them in a vase half-filled with yearning and likes looking at them anyway. Her mouth leaves traces of soil on the stamp.

Untitled

Aurielle Destiche

Your face buckles
as if it's you leaving
this world you created,
not us.

This world where only we
know you, remember you:
your witch's cry,
your hungry mouth
gleaming for a woman.

You turn back in earnest
just before the tree line,
darkness pressing your eyes.
But it's too late. We have withered
into gas.

Night sewn up
tight between the firs—
their spires
showing us the way out.

Cassia

Gina Ferrara

The proliferation will make you swallow
intentions, uncontrollable and punctuated.
You will interrogate the falsely pious,
anyone who tries to suppress by uprooting
and will not applaud the unabashed
cascading always in November
closer to goldenrod then saffron.
In silent avalanches, the unadulterated
proclaims itself through pure color.
The planter remains unknown,
anonymous, a previous occupant
with a shovel that struck dirt along the fence,
giving terrain to your only horizon, duplicated
somewhere south of a place never visited,
brought today by the bend and spray in descent,
untamed flowers you hesitate to name or prune—
every petal steeped with the promise of something better
as your fingers pull apart braided trilogies of branches.

Another Broken Curfew

Gina Ferrara

Since I left the intricacy
of what had been wrought

in the corner, the sheer gauze,
a gossamer, newly formed,

fly away filaments, a sheen of uncertainty,
headlights illuminating,

illuminating my mother spectral and epic
in the doorway, she stood barefoot.

A pain came with my arrival—
maybe she felt the first jolt,

uncanny, nearly electric,
the noise almost levitating her

one hour before the sky became unstuck;
my mother heard the engine

each cylinder annunciating
then backfiring, the audacity,

the wheezing, the rough idle
on the verge of undulating,

the boy departing in dawn's direction
with only the two syllables of his name.

That Voice

Gina Ferrara

For Nason Smith

I told you once about country music,
the way it reminded me of a one-eyed cat
and sizable rust spots on a metal pail,

busted carburetors leaking oily pools filled
with happenstance iridescence, how most of it
made me want to scream, to self-annihilate

to just surrender when it was time for a fight,
the tales of loving til the day after forever
from the depths of a cell or distillation measured in years.

No glee or joy came from telling you
that your idol was dead, your legend,
Merle, whose own mamma said

he was, as a child, incorrigible,
capable of stretching elastic to eternity,
whose voice you heard with or without revolutions

holding the exact cadence and conditions
of half-patched threadbare brothers and the father
you wouldn't bring yourself to bury.

The Pink Orange

Amelia Cook Fontella

After Chernobyl, she sat beside her new husband,
his hair in clumps on the pillow like fallen baby birds,
body crumbling like burned paper in water: first blisters,
then dust. One day he had the orange for her, a gift,
on his bedside table, the one that was big and pink,
the one he wanted her to eat, because she loved oranges.

How can we describe love? The taste of oranges
in winter? The wife who cannot fall asleep, the husband
who holds her hand? Cold skin flushed pink
alongside the fire? These days I dream not enough of birds
and too much of snakes, weddings are more about gift
than give, and my heart is padded in blisters.

And then, on the radio, this story retold: the boils and blisters,
the way the woman saw beauty in them, how oranges
were the only thing he had for her, how she accepted the gift
even though it was poison, how when her husband
slept she whispered "I love you," how those words were birds
that landed on her shoulders, and stained her cheeks pink.

And the orange he gave her, she called it pink
and I don't understand why, the way I don't understand how blisters
fill with water and break open, how every winter birds
find their warm homes in trees with branches decorated in oranges
like Christmas bulbs. I have not yet married, never had a husband
who would give me everything, even if fruit was his only gift.

But the orange had been too close to him, a gift
that would kill her, and the nurses waved their pink
fingers through the glass. He's no longer your husband,
they mouthed, he's nothing more than bones and blisters,
and nothing can save him: not holding him, not eating oranges.
He cannot hear you, your voice is senseless as chirping birds.

She carried his tray and stayed next to him, told him of the birds
outside the window, the way a crushed worm was a gift
and small sticks made up nests, their throats like oranges,
bellies red as cherry jam, their babies wrinkled and pink.
Her legs were swollen from staying awake, her heels grew blisters
from walking the floor, but she couldn't stop loving her husband.

The wife and husband are gone now. Here, it's spring and pink
flowers are pushing up, the sunsets are soft as oranges, power lines fill
with birds.
The blisters on my feet from a walk around the lake are a gift.

Immigrant

Amelia Cook Fontella

I move toward you
like a lit village

full of strangers tending fires
in early night, on the edge

of jungle, in a country I do not know,
but recognize.

November 2nd

Amelia Cook Fontella

Crushed marigolds at my feet
petals like orange pulp.
Their seeds: black toothpicks with tiny tufts of white.
The altars have been taken down,
disappeared like the dead while we slept.

MEDITATIONS AT MONTEGUT:
A Rethinking of *Blackberry*

Kelly Gartman

All of the new thinking is about easy gain.
In this way it resembles all of the old thinking.
The idea, for example, that one image can clarify
the confusion of an entire decade. That a clown-
faced gutterpunk probing the sculpted wreck
of a Volkswagen bus is, by his presence, some tragic falling
off from a first world filled with unlimited high-interest credit cards.
Or the other notion that, because there is in this world
no one good thing to which the cadence of "dirtbag" corresponds,
the logos is the lone elegy to that which it signifies.

We spoke about it late last night. In the tone
of my dirtbag friend, there was a thin rat-a-tat
of recognition, a sound almost intelligent.
After a while I realized that, in talking this way
with him, everything in me dissolves: patience,
civility, the will to go on. There was a man
I hurt and I remember how, holding
his narrow shoulders in my hands,
I felt a violent spasm of nausea
like a desperate thirst for peace,
for my past remade with its barrier
islands of hope, tragic music
from the Carnival boats, and dangerous, humid places
where we caught mudbugs called fish.
It hardly had to do with him, or anyone.

Longing, we call it, only because desire is so weary
of endless short distances. I am not the same now
and I want to remember little—the way his hands
dismantled beer cans, the thing his father did
that hurt him, what he said. There are moments
when the heart is as mysterious as forgotten words

and days that are merely a cacophony of sweat and flesh
relentlessly hulking forward. Such despair,
such despondency in those blistering August evenings,
lying on a sagging mattress under a slow fan, muttering
dirtbag, dirtbag, dirtbag.

Omertà

Anne Marie Giovingo

(My father remembers when he was eight)

Uncle Dominic
lifted me into the wagon
and led me down
to the house where nobody lived. He said, "Sshhh,
listen,
for sounds in the woods."
He said, "Wait here,
while I go get some things somebody *uh-*
bandoned." I listened
to the *swish* of the pines in the wind.
I listened to the *chip* of the cardinals,
to the noise the mockingbirds made. I heard
a crow. . . far off
a pig squealed.
I heard Uncle Dominic
curse the things
he could not see
inside the house.
He called out,
"Do you hear
anything?" I said,
No.
"No need," he said,
as he loaded the wagon,
"to tell your Mamma
where we went today.
Your Mamma and me,
we see things different."
No, I said.
Different,
the way
Mamma makes us eat berries the birds peck,

saving the best ones for the baskets,
three rows of three on top,
each one fat and resting on three leaves,
like baby birds in a nest.
Different,
the way
Uncle Dominic
crouches low
in the field
to eat the best berries,
hot and juicy right from the vines, then hides
the pecked ones
in baskets with straw
underneath.

Woods

Anne Marie Giovingo

for Enza

This evening we pass through
what remains of the ancient forest
on our way from Bisaquino
in the Provence of Palermo
to Sambuca, the venerable
town and home of the newly invented
pizza topped with fries.
As in a scene from a Frank Capra production,
the light fades,
our road twists to become
too dark for us
to distinguish the trees.
Quick fox and quicker rabbit
evoke the royal hunts,
evade the car's lights.
What we don't know of the past
or can't bear to remember
makes us imagine
a lost history as lyrical as the game the children play
in the back seat of the car:
carta, forbici, pietra—
paper, scissors, rock,
their intense and insistent chant
lulling us into a waking sleep.
What their game recalls,
what these hills cause us to remember,
fills the air with plenty.

Epigenetics

Jeff Grieneisen

Maybe we are the people
of our heritage,
the past distilled
into reaction.

Above the genome
memories swirl like flocks of birds
seeking entrance. Memory,
the collected interpretation,
tries to survive, to enter our bodies
and drill down to our children.
This body, an empty vessel to be filled
with bits of memory, electrical impulses,
or chemicals,
encoded on that spiral staircase of DNA,
changing us,

and I can I feel my grandfather
leaning onto the breast auger,
drilling a hole in shale large enough
to hold the charge.
Today, his hand guides mine
over the open frame of true 2x4s in the cellar.

Where do I get the urge to drink? To scratch
out words on these pages,
to tell the stories
as if they've been gathering
in this body for generations?
Scots fled to Ireland fled
to Pennsylvania, USA.
We like to have our heritages,
like inherited yearning for potatoes
or bad tempers.

At Emory University school of Medicine,
scientists found mice
can pass on learned information
about traumatic or stressful experiences
to subsequent generations.
The mouse child or grandchild
does not know why he cowers and runs
from scent of cherry blossom.

Experiences transfer
brain to genome:
a spider-fright on the boat from Castelluccio
at the turn of the century,
and my wife now has no ability to sit beside one,
curds and whey or not.

Body and Soul

Jeff Grieneisen

When the Apache helicopter
my wife's cousin flew
crashed
or was shot down
in Afghanistan, they recovered
seventy pounds of body,

bits and pieces carried off the field
in a bag sagging with the weight of flesh
equal to:
10 human hearts
7 medium bowling balls
7 large bags of flour
A healthy 10-year-old girl.

Seventy pounds of unattached flesh
lie in the coffin
before which we all knelt

in solemn prayer
for speedy service of his soul—
to reach the heights
we know the soul must reach.

The body left behind for us
rolled through country roads,
a hero saluted in small towns
by families holding flags.

What's left, DNA-tested, matched to a test sample,

gathered, as if the fact of flesh matters,
whose remains, real flesh, lie in repose
to be prayed for/prayed over.

We need to honor that the flesh is in there,
that we are praying for the right body
even though the soul probably lifted already
over Afghan mountains.

Radioactive

Matt Groneman

It splits our core, this elemental change,
each time iambs turn radium to radon.
Images spin around our nuclei
and madly threaten to break off, arrange
us into ions, short us one electron,
and then we'll all be atoms gone awry.

Yes, strophes change the human condition,
allusion interconnecting neural nodes
until we are a double-helix. Encode
the mind of Oppenheimer. His decision
was this: to build the bomb and drop the lode
when lines could put our ethos on a collision
course where words sear and brand our souls through fission
as permanent as the genetic code.

Hot August Night

Matt Groneman

As an infant, I took Neil Diamond very seriously,
listening to *Hot August Night* while lying snug in my crib.
Later, he went Vegas, and I turned smug, the casino glitz
keeping me away for far too long. When I started
listening again, I knew why it was *this* album I fell asleep to.

But now, it wasn't quite déjà vu. Instead of sleep,
I wanted to leap, shout. I had found myself again.
I popped up in the cowpoke comedy that filled side two
of four. I am the forsaken, old carpenter
crafting for no one in "Morningside." I can
at least appreciate "Done Too Soon's" impulse
to attempt to simultaneously empathize
with Jesus Christ, Ho Chi Minh and that American
Judas, John Wilkes Booth, all in the same verse.

And I'm there again on the album cover—
the way Neil looks so lost. Distraught, he stands
staring down into the void
between his hands. He is handling our hamartia—
that paralytic fear that when we step to the brink
we will realize the future is sprawling, a nebulae
of the unknowable. All we can do is prepare
for the performative catharsis that must soon follow.

9:30

Matt Groneman

That was when we heard the garage door.
Mom began reheating the meatloaf.
Ten minutes later you stumbled in
sloshing a tumbler of box wine and stinking—a surprise,
since you didn't smoke. You clutched the kitchen
counter, felt your way across the floor
until you found mom, then groped her
while she tried to brush you off. One violent wobble
and you shuffled off to the bedroom, cursing
her under your breath
as you went to change out of your suit.

The meatloaf warmed, mom screamed
toward the back of the house, then sent me
to find you. After a few rounds
of yelling down the hallway
(no one believed you were half deaf
and you couldn't hear us at all
when we found out we'd been wrong),
I huffed back to your bedroom.

I didn't see you
at first. I thought you had slipped
out the front door and back to the bar, stung
by the guilt of making yourself unwelcome.
You were there though, and when I turned around I felt you—
or at least your elbow—as it brushed against my heel.
You had fallen
asleep, drunk and drooly, on the closet floor.
You lay there, curled in the fetal position,
wearing only your thin black socks.

Washing his Dead Ex-Girlfriend

Kia Groom

’s clothes seems futile. dead girls don’t wear
jeans, don’t care about the stink. but here
she is—a couple of pairs of graying
panties & some thrift
store finds, bundled in a Wal-Mart bag.

i don’t think about the body. i measure
detergent in a plastic cap, wonder
about softener. in this house
laundry is my calling.
i do it exceptionally well. i do it
so it feels like forgetting. i do it
so it feels surreal.

the agitator churns, drowns
out the re-play. his voice
on the phone, the way it snapped
like a limb: *she’s what!?*

i never heard her
voice but through the chambers
i hear it tumbling, a high
thin keen. ghost wail. maybe
a song. would she like that?

when he came
home he made me try it
on—*this one is pretty cool*—a ghoulish
cat face on a black silk
shirt & i thought how she and i
had almost touched twice now;

fabric and third party skin
like we could have been sisters.

The Other Girls Fall Through Me

Kia Groom

like a dye diffusion—vibrate
my core like a chalk circle.

The other girls are root
system. They are collateral
damage.

The other girls fuse their cellular debris
to my wind-up meat vehicle.

The other girls are coming
for my crystal core.

The other girls echo in my hollows—sluice
over me like chlorine baptism.

They are every girl. They are no
girl ever.

The other girls invoke their lipstick omens
inside my pulsing halls.

The other girls are a chronology of hauntings,
they spell me like backwards taxidermy.

They weave their fractured polaroids
into my small intestine. They make me
a gallery of dislocated crime.

They repeat me
                    repeat me
like bad
                    bad
proverbs—reverse me like antidotes.

The other girls are a digestion
of arcane language—they verb me like noun.

I am like the other
girls but I am not—I am not—I am
not those girls.

Their hands are grabbing / I am
grabbing their hands. They are not
visible / I am
coming up in welts / miracle
rash I am / coming
under my skin / .The other
girls are a blessing / a highway
I walk down the other / girls are
coming to a crescendo, coming
to a white hot
peak they are
coming to an occult /
fever they are
coming to a bruised moon
/ socket they are
coming they are
coming I am
coming I
am coming
I am
coming
I
am
coming
for the other
girls.

PRE-TEEN PYTHIA

Kia Groom

I am the moon-bruised, glitter-mouthed
middle-school medium! Fist-full
of promo-prophylactics,
board burned in the bleachers
with Playboy Zippo. Give me
a gum stick, a cigarette, a neon gel pen. I've got a line
to the dead & all your demons.
I've got a vulva so haunted
I wove panties from dried sage. My aura is well
lubricated. Hold my hand.
The condom wrapper says I LOVE U & I
don't. Tear it anyway. Pop out the purple
latex. Place two fingers on the rim & watch
it slip-slide over alphabet. My eyes may roll
into blue-webbed lash clumps: clairvoyance
or contempt. Of course you want
an A on the final, a hot
prom date. Of course you want
to bother spirits with your half-limp dick.
The ghosts in my cell walls speak
in riddles, don't care for your nervous
probes. Splayed
apart like this it's easy
to forget the difference between plump sun
YES & wasted lunar
NO. I catch
a breath. Third eye wince. But this
is it, my magic
flesh, my slick trance state.

Watch for omens. Look between.
I do nothing & still
the planchette moves.

I am the Tin Boy, yes it's true

Wren Hanks

I am the Tin Boy, yes it's true.
Witness, I wash off my Dorothy sheen,
take the contacts out (eyes still mineral blue)
& expose my washboard ridges,
offer you the sexiness of my metal
to fleck inside your mouth.
(Witness, I'll kiss you like a real boy would.)

Witness me ma'amed during our dinner date,
the emerald light magnifying your acne &
my oh-so-delicate hands.
Lean on me, Witness, in the alleyway,
my raw-puce-velvet heart
leaking sawdust on your tits.

Witness, call me *good sport*, shimmy off my suit
& excavate my girly blood bag.
Pin me, shove a silver slipper against
my throat to keep me honest.
(I'll preen for you, I can't help myself.)

Witness me tin cry until my boy-lashes melt:
No one, Polychrome, had to teach me this shame.

"The key to open up tomorrow is reality"

Wren Hanks

My ghosts see me clearly as a charred tree line. I'm a cat in a surgery lab whose spine's been severed. I'm a boy with a vigorous hair flip. I'm a boy with burning hair & the cerulean eyes of romance heroes. You've stopped believing me now, but the ghosts bring me super soakers to fight the neighbors, long since gendered & grown up. You've stopped believing me now, but I'm the one in the story with hands for eyes. The fir tree rustling with ash.

My bravest ghost splits open at the chest, offers me a duelist's sword like we're in an episode of *Revolutionary Girl Utena*. You've stopped believing me now, but I'll cut a Midnight Supreme off your bustier. Toss my velvet hair and claim a scorched & empty win.

I'm not kissing girls who have to get / blitzed / to touch me

Wren Hanks

I'm not I'm not I'm not / It's not true she wants / something different from me / than her boyfriend / Or it is / and that's hell too / she gets on her knees / on the dance floor / she presses her face against my hip / I'm supposed to pretend my body feels nothing / I know that / next time I'll say / my confusing body feels nothing / my traitor body feels nothing / put your hand in my jeans and see how much nothing I feel

I will / I'll say it / not / I'm wet & hard & still not real / enough / for you I won't say / I'm a good boy / enough-boy / a spit-curl-you-could-pull-when-I'm-sucking-your-clit boy / I'm dry I'll say / I'm chalk I'll say / pull off a limb and it'll grow back I'll say / but nothing / she tips back her head / the whiskey on her breath / the ginger on her breath / like a sea star / I'm brainless / I won't I won't I won't / move closer / her palm against my chest now / my sweating crushed ant chest now / just take another shot I'll say / just leaving me standing here I'll say / just go home with that girl / that boy I try / to say / before her drunk / her confident cis tongue / is in my mouth

The Minotaur

Jade Hurter

When I was born I cracked my mother to the sternum. She bled for days, and when they sewed her up she was never the same, said Father: a woman cut in half, though she'd always been a woman divided. I suckled until she cut me off, with blades fit against her nipples. My sliced mouth dripped over the breakfast table, rust in the milky tea, I couldn't hold my fork for shaking. When I got older I didn't fit on the bus, so I walked to school, clip-clopping along the pavement. The kids all liked my hooves, but they never asked me over for birthday cake or pool parties. Father would watch me do homework in the afternoons, his eyes dark slits. I cried when Mother was at work, cried when she came home and smacked the tough hide of my backside. You're a monster, she told me. Act like it. When other children turned thirteen, their parents threw them parties at the roller rink. I heard them talking about it in the cafeteria, but of course no one made skates for feet like mine. I turned thirteen and Mother put me out of the house. She left me to sleep in the garden, to eat the scraps of toast and orange peel Father left on the windowsill each evening. I got used to it. The crickets, the jays, the passionvine that twisted around my horns as I slept. I picked caterpillars off the sweet olive, grew dizzy with the smell of orange blossom. Soon I began to pull out the weeds, to clip the rosebushes into hedges, until I had fashioned a verdant maze. In the center, it was so quiet. I only wanted to be alone.

Still Life

Jade Hurter

In which I hold a piece of quartz
    between my thumb and forefinger

In which the roots of waterlily
    hang suspended in my throat

In which I hold a knife
    to a whistling duck's dark neck

In which white ibis are stuck
    like maggots to my body

In which I pick them off, one by one
    to reveal glowing wounds

In which I wear a crown of orange bills,
    curving inward like tusks

In which my belly is swollen with egret blood,
    though you cannot tell from looking

In which I am a sculpture of feathers,
    dipping my palms in the river

In which I hold a knife—

Leda & the Swan

Jade Hurter

I guess you've heard that swans are violent creatures. Reptile-shapes fallen asleep in the snow and awakened shining. So I don't have to tell you that when I was young, I was attacked by a swan, large and screaming. It was nesting season, thick spring, pink jelly raindrops alighting in the pond nearby. The swan rose before me, marshmallow soft, neck twisting like taffy, took my dark wings in its black beak and tore.

Eyes fell from my feathers, scattered like pearls. It swallowed all but two like hard candy. The swan ripped me open, dug golden dust from behind my ribs, swallowed my second heart still-beating. It licked the blue fur from my body, left me naked as a shucked oyster. The swan became a cloud. Its white wings dark the sky.

And this, you know, is how girls are made.

The day I gave up drinking

Samantha Isasi

Here's the thing.
        I didn't mean to.
One night, I just did a reverse Jesus
and drank water with dinner instead of wine.
Oh, come on,
that's funny, not blasphemous.
No, I never considered myself to have
a "problem."
Yes, those are air quotes.
God, I know, I hate fuckers who use those things, too.
The next night, I was watching TV, and I just didn't really think about it.
Then, I realized
it had been a week.
I felt like I had been betraying my people.
No, not the Jews.
The drinkers.
And now? Well, now I just feel useless.
Look at this glass of stupid water. I'm useless and healthy and sober.
I don't even feel like drinking. I might live for fucking ever.
I may as well start going to the gym.

Towards Goodbye

Samantha Isasi

I am trying to grow an avocado from its pit
and my dog is dying.

I am making popcorn
a movie paused on the television
and my dog is dying.

The avocado pit is splitting from the center
suspended in a cup of water on the windowsill
by four toothpicks.
Does my dog know
her fate has been decided?

I am splitting through the middle
and salting the popcorn
and spraying butter
and my dog is dying.
And I have to set a date for her to die.

The avocado absorbs water
more quickly now that it has broken apart.
And my dog is lying in her bed
in front of the artificial blue glow
and I hand my daughter the bowl.
When she presses play,
the sound covers my dog's bare breathing.

The Sky Isn't Blue

Kelly Jones

In North Carolina, even though there are songs about it,
and late night arguments in bars about the shade
of a shirt or the rallying
cry of a drunken sports enthusiast,
the sky isn't blue. The sky
isn't blue anywhere, it is a spectrum,
a wave of colors that our eyes can't process.
Today I left work early
because I felt inexplicably dizzy.
I walked outside and saw the world tinged yellow.
The ground moved under my feet and I felt floaty
as pollen in spring, ready to wash away in the next storm.
Tomorrow is May Day and there is a protest downtown.
Meet me on the corner, at the edge of the crowd,
by the wildflowers. Bring a brick
that is perfect for shattering glass.
The sky isn't any different here, but I am.

When I said I wanted to live

Kelly Jones

better than we were, I didn't mean fancy things. I didn't
mean a new car or lunches at expensive restaurants.

I didn't mean change, of course, but adventure.
Or freedom. I think I meant I wanted to move to the desert,

and leave everything behind in the past,
where nostalgia makes it more beautiful.

I am strong but sentimental. I still have a jar of sand
a friend gave me twenty years ago. It's darkened

to a nasty brown and yet still I hold onto it.
Youth is hard to let go of. Remember my face

when you met me? It was flush with whiskey
and possibility. We were winding down

a crowded street on Halloween, costumed
and full of confidence. It was a great parade,

but when it ended I found myself frightened
by the people passing by with makeup running

down their faces. There are creases around my eyes
and glitter from yesterday. From tomorrow.

When I am gone, I hope the obit is simple and true:
She sparkled and moved and she seethed with irreverence.

Aubade for November 9th, 2016

Kelly Jones

Let me wake

slowly in the dim
light mourning
this morning

in a different world

tangled in satin sheets
in a bed that holds the shape
of his body

where the dead wait

to say *you should have known better*
while offering condolences

for the future

apologies we'll make
for this mistake, make
no sudden moves,
this bomb is set

to explode

all it'll take is a tiny
itchy finger to push
the button and wait
for the very best
show ever
to unfold

like the folds

    of a woman
    begging to be
    grabbed – or just walking by
    outside and out

of time

Wallace Stevens's Secretary

Ginny Kaczmarek

> *Stevens took to composing poems on slips of paper*
> *in the morning while walking to his office,*
> *where his secretary typed them up.*
> —*The New Yorker,* May 2, 2016

Less muse than conduit, I fail to feel his phrases
through my fingertips. Who tastes the emperor's ice cream,

anyway? Black ink slams white letterhead at 90 wpm—
sign, seal, send, then on to settlements. My inbox overflows;

one more *Take a memo, Sweetheart* and I'll bust.
Every anecdote illuminates his jar in my field,

no matter what wilderness I welcome in myself.

Lego Day at the Children's Museum

Ginny Kaczmarek

One green, one orange, twin towers lean
precariously. Twin girls, brows blanched,

stack Legos above their heads. Watching, I wonder,
Do they know?

                                        Eleven years ago today,

before you kids were born, airplanes tore
a blue September morning: the crash

and after. Flames bloomed from windows,
useless alarms cried on and on, and people

tumbled to the ground.

                                        To brace collapsing towers,
intrepid kids gather blocks, babbling

about joining forces.

                                        No, children, go home.
Chicken Little was right: the sky has fallen.

Project complete, the girls pose. Flash—
they're gone. The towers remain intact

until   *crash*   children shatter stacks,
collect the pieces, and build something new.

Lament

Ginny Kaczmarek

for Helen Hill, filmmaker, activist, wife, mother, friend murdered in her New Orleans home January 4, 2007

A bullet's callous fury found my friend
and I admit my shame: I love this city,
the murder capital of America.
Helen, we shared a dream: to build our homes
among cicada song, oak-lined streets, lace
and iron. We dreamt children, music, art;
we thought that we would die here, entombed
in sun-bleached alabaster under oaks—
but not like that, shot in the neck, pleading,
Please don't hurt my baby, helpless, bleeding.

Your death shocked us awake, we who remain;
levees of privilege failed to barricade
blood from Uptown. We marched in rage and love,
our loss absorbed by sultry morning air,
demanding: Do you thirst or weep, New Orleans,
when gunshots drown our voices, ink spills names
of the dead, and mourners clog the streets,
parades of shame unable to move forward?

A bullet found my friend; my hands drip red.
What have I done to stem the tide but cry
for her, for all of us whose blood still flows
through streets to thirsty earth, to the river
that drains this country's sludge. River, hear me
above the languid drone of apathy:
Cleanse our wretched city cutting lives
like blades of grass. Be sated. Thirst no more.

Helen, your voice haunts dreams, begs *please*
don't hurt my baby, fills my mouth with pleas

for my son. He's two, the same as yours
the day you died. How do we keep them safe
when random bits of lead cleave mornings
into *before* and *after*?
          Paul and Francis
moved far away from city ghosts, but we
remained, my family and me. We watch
your movie *Mouseholes*, listen to your songs;
your hopeful voice fills rooms, allays our fear
here, where your quirky heart bloomed into art,
here, where a bullet claimed your life, here, where
we revel in your dreams dancing on screens.
The movie ends; my son says, "More," and yes,
Helen, we wanted more from you, these films
keep ending. We rewind to hear you sing
here, where we live, New Orleans, our home.

Strolling on the Rambla in Barcelona

Andrew Kindiger

after Miró

A heart, a flash of blue, in the mind,
an object outside reality—an endless street,
a depthless sea. A desire to dream
captured in each step.
The world is disfigured
with passersby, those who say hello,
those who don't.

People are pressed into a portrait by the eye—
a splash of color surrounding
an opal breast, a cloudy leg, each impression
is hued by nuance, by white space, warmed
in every glance, in the glow
of the blood orange disk.

Order

Andrew Kindiger

Sweet conclusion, we do not
always know why we've met.

Often there is little to do except
wait to paint the chaos.

As you return my notes, I'd rather
my haste be met with understanding.

I will caution against the apparent
and attempt to seek stillness.

I will demand quiet as my mind
confronts distraction.

If there must always be regret,
I will remain patient.

The Meat Eater

Nate Kostar

She said,
I'm a vegetarian because the treatment of animals in this country
appalls me.
He said,
I'm a meat eater because the taste of animals in this country delights
me.
She said,
Do you know how many hormones they pump into chickens so that
we fat Americans will be happy?
He said,
No.

The waiter came.

She said,
I'll have the vegetable dumplings and mixed vegetable soup. Thank
you.
He said,
Sesame chicken, pork fried rice, and a side of boneless spare ribs.
Thank you.
She said,
Do you realize a chicken, pig, and cow were killed so you could have
one meal?
He said,
Do you realize a man, woman, and child were killed for your
"freedom?"
She said,
No.

They ate in silence until

He said,
With every bite I hear their cries. The chickens are clucking,
piggies squealing, cows moooo—

She said,
You're a fucking asshole.

He smiled.
She smiled.
They laughed.

He leaned forward to kiss her.

She said,
Eww! Your breath stinks!
He said,
It's their *souls.*

Coliseum Park

Nate Kostar

I.

You should see the place the Saint was murdered,
on the late night when the birds are chirping,
and jasmine petals hug the ground, like snowflakes
holding yellow secrets in their mouths,

gently kissed on pavement cheeks—eyelashes,
while dewdrops flash on distant leaves
like cameras down on Bourbon Street
or sun-bounced waves beside a beach—

through the dark in spring, tonight, after rain's
come down to soak the city through the ground,
the sky so low and wet it sags like laundry in a cotton bag,
the air a bathroom sponge, and every atom wags its juicy tongue—

an orange night, or black and gold, true story told,
the lanterns hang against the mansions where the blues were sung,
but now is home to new and young who come
and come from all the places that they're from,

and gather here to walk their dogs,
to talk in coffee shops and restaurants and bars,
even a park where children play, beside a road
where people on their way to work pass by in cars.

II.

You should see the place the Saint was murdered,
on the late night when the birds are chirping,
and stay to watch the glow of early morning
when the sky turns pink, blood-red and orange—

oh! how beautiful to see the dawn
on the block that he was on
when the gun was drawn
and he was gone.

But then it hits when I walk past,
the black and gold, the teammates
smiling, the family pictures
hanging on the fence.

Even the air has a certain smell.
Is it new or was it always here?

As I listen to New Orleans like a song,
a siren plays the keys, unseen birds hit notes,
a steamboat moans and distant cars make loops;
a subtle canvas for this evening's slow-drawn harmonies,

and something feels so soft tonight,
and still, and strange,
but stranger still,
still perfect.

Pantoum of the Pack

Cat Lautenbach

We traveled long distances together.
With the dogs, we walked in all weather.
Though we always ended where we started,
we never took the same steps twice.

With the dogs, we walked in all weather,
in varying shades of light.
We never took the same steps twice.
Cold snaps would ignite our pace.

In varying shades of light,
our shadows would sometimes overlap.
Cold snaps would ignite our pace.
We watched the dogs trot through grass.

Our shadows would sometimes overlap
as if we were extensions of each other.
We watched the dogs trot through grass
and considered our next steps.

As if we were extensions of each other,
when one of us stopped, we all stopped
and considered our next steps.
If one of us couldn't walk, we'd carry him.

When one of us stopped, we all stopped.
We wouldn't go on without each other.
If one of us couldn't walk, we'd carry him
through rain, heat, and the pain of grief.

We wouldn't go on without each other.
Though we always ended where we started,
through rain, heat, and the pain of grief,
we traveled long distances together.

The Gift of an Asparagus Fern

Cat Lautenbach

First, the theft of the asparagus fern
made us realize why we love this plant:
a Sprengeri, esteemed for its evergreen
resilience. The perennial shrugs off a chill,
won't wilt in heat, and on some local grounds,
grows like a weed, which makes it difficult
to understand the intentions of the thief,
or thieves (as our plant was huge,
lifting it may have required two
stealthy reapers to cart it off).

Then all that remained of our mighty fern
was a damp plate-sized spot on the cement slab
where its planter sat capping a porch pillar.
We'd raised it as a living monument to mark
our entrance to the sacred spot we call home.
Its crown was almost four feet in diameter; its stalks
grew as long tendrils draping down the stairs.

I disagreed with the police
who called the crime of its departure
petty. We had carried pitchers of water to it
every Saturday and Wednesday
for fifteen years. I'd gladly sweep up,
for fifteen more, the fern's discarded and drifting
cladodes—those needle-like leaves of its foliage
that when left loose followed us inside and out—
a small price to pay for all this plant was to us:

a large green shield that, in its full display,
blocked the sight of a leaky fire hydrant
and the crumbling curb alongside it;
a charm that lured song birds to us
in spring with its lacy white flowers

and dangling red berries; a humble host
that responded to all our rushed comings and goings
with a welcome wave and a gentle sway.

We greeted our neighbors with lament
over the loss, saying, "If only we'd put it down
in some cob-webbed corner, then
thieves would not have found it." We went on,
"If only we didn't care for it, it would've blended in
with the street and its potholes." They nodded.

The empty spot on the porch remained
vacant in memory of the missing fern.
We carried all our other plants
to the backyard. If thieves were to return,
we would not make it easy for them
to take the cactus rose or the sister fern.
Although we vowed to steel our hearts,
it felt impossible for us to stop caring.
We wanted to protect our plants, I mean,
ourselves. Somehow we'd poured ourselves
into these pots and planters,
and into other pretty things we love
to place around us. So, we fortified ourselves
and wondered if thieves were watching.

Then one morning, on the swept
and otherwise empty porch,
a young asparagus fern appeared
planted in dark soil in a small terra-cotta pot.
We almost overlooked it, but the movement
of our feet caused its sprigs of sprout green
to sway and catch our sight. There,
in our shadows, the simple plant stood
as the essence of care,
as the fruit of a neighbor's empathy,
as the embodiment of resilience.
Our Sprengeri had found a way

to come back after its theft as a gift.
It returned as quietly as it had left,
and, as if from pruning after a frost,
it came back fresh and rejuvenated.
Then we understood completely
why we love this plant.

Jubilee

Cat Lautenbach

With deep circles of debt under my eyes,
I see only glowing numbers in a dark room.
The clock shows how silently time can move:
without even a tick for what seems like fifty
years served motionless. I imagine God wants
to save me, first, with a vision; then I will hear
the sound of heavenly armies marching in.
I wonder how the allergy medicine I took
will affect my dreaming.

I dream of all my friends and family dancing
in the VFW hall. Grandpa and all his brothers
swing their sisters in a jittery rock-step twirl.
My cousins pull me into their circle
to move in sync with them; first, we chitter-chatter
with our hands, then flap our elbows before we shake
our tail feathers: we dance like chickens.
And for the next song, we sing along with our arms
spelling out *the Y-M-C-A*. Everyone bounces
and nods with grins and smiles. Old friends
are young again and point approvingly to my freestyle
kicks and jabs. I haven't seen any of these people
in such a long while, but I still know them intimately.
They gather to celebrate with me; this is my party.

No one sweats. None of us need a break, yet
the DJ still mixes in a slow love song,
which brings together my mom and brother.
They cry rejoicing in each other's arms
when they see my father and me trying
to give it a whirl. I step all over his feet
and muffle my laughter in his suit jacket sleeve.
He's much more tolerant than I remember,
and he looks his best, as we all do, so finely dressed.

Soon the music is less sentimental:
It's time to celebrate and have a good time.
My mom twists with Grandma and spins
her around; they laugh and bump their hips
together. What a riotous romping joy—this Jubilee!
With all, at last, restored, the trumpets blast.

The alarm goes off. As fingers of light reach
into the room, I rise with hopes of going home.

In the wild

Jesse Loren

She does better
A foxhole, a food supply—

An equality of unknowns
without the tenets of oppression.

Does the male always do better?
Challenging the wiser antelope?
Or shifting his gender to hers as needed?

My neighbor used to say dogs belonged in the yard.
Like bunnies, or songbirds, his knowledge
Filled in by his father.

His Chi-Chi shivered and scratched
Her paws, like finches tapping on the door
Until like a leaf, her life cord snapped and the
Curled shell, dusted with snow, hardened on the porch

In the wild
Of Iowa, fields and flatness
She flew out, sailed across the sky like a witch
As the car rolled and curled into its shell

All along the cornfield, her teeth—
The very fabric of her clothes torn off
  by the force of hurling through space and fear
  landing, as the cord snapped,
  Her fur matted with her own blood
                                                            For a time
The tops of the corn stocks shook, then they didn't.
Corn, like all the rock and dirt, silent as pinnacles
pointing her skyward.

I imagine the pieces of her, like pomegranate seeds
Spread on the ground, in leaves, on the blond ovary hairs of the corn,
On the back of sow bugs rolled and opening.

In the wild,
I would know
In her feet, a sisterhood, repeating,
  "I am here, I am alive. Please find me."
Iowa.

For Vorticism

Jesse Loren

And the blue was bluer than the triune blue of the Dauphin.
Bluer than plums
Bluer than the sunlight on the obelisk or
a call to prayer.
Cobalt, cyanine, impalpable truths.

One can set keel to breakers here.
One can set a poem in paper and float it
across the azure, the webbed mist, the clear cornflower.

The Brandeis not the cerulean. I have seen it emptied
And full.
The Dodger
The Yale, the teal all woven together like nets.

I have seen the laughter of brides over turquoise rings.

Here, the ell-shaped pitkin had been dug, the rock, quarried,
libation upon libation poured and woven into ropes.

Here the hole gone under, a Hieratic head buried in memory
Like the town, the grain, the tombstone.

Sigismundo, Malatesta.

Prussian too,
An escape velocity.
Another Henri Gaudier.
The howling and baying for their mothers
Pulling down, down, down,
all down into an open maw.
Old Wyndham Lewis was lost too, like Elpenor, he missed a step.
Nobody would want his eyes…

A vortex, begging, spaghettification,
A lonely volcano greater than a singularity.
A mirror
A pit.

Wurstfest, New Braunfels, 11/9/2016

Maya Lowy

Here's masses of Texans in twenty-buck
hats: hats with buttons on, Viking hats, poop
emoji hats, hats that look like chickens.

The bars in here primarily carry
Shiner & Bud Light, but one's got German
beers: Spaten & Hofbrau, Paulaner &
Dunkel, color-coded so the girl who
takes my order just has to holler, Can
I get a Small Green & grab my ticket.

Alex Meixner, virtuoso on the
accordion, headlines the set tonight.
A couple folks can actually polka.
The crowd is raucous, cheering in German,
but organized & polite. Nobody
mentions the election; the closest thing
to politics here is the bratwurst stand
tip jar labeled for Chloe's college fund.

I'm sharing a footlong brat on a stick
with my sister, who has never been to
Texas before. Last night when I tried to
open my window it broke clean in three
big pieces.

April 26, 1973:

Maya Lowy

To think we've been living here so peacefully with that laying in the ground.

On overcast Ord Street
the fog burns off
by afternoon

trout season opens Saturday
whales, dolphins, surfers
bob below the cliffs

I Dream of Jeannie's
on Channel 8, *Star Trek*
on Channel 2

the meat boycott
means everybody cooks
tofu curries, mushroom frittatas

and sixteen
inches below
they dig up

a ten-pound
head
that was once Cindy's

and couldn't have taken long to bury. Packed loam has settled in the ears, the nostrils. The eyes must have pointed right at him as he shoveled. He left them open: dirt settled against them, worms found them firm and supple. Cloudy eyeballs flattened and blank, mouth ajar, eyes pointed right at him. And Cindy could see nothing. She was gone, that thing just a husk that had once been hers. Cindy was gone. She was fog and nothing he did now could hurt her. The dismantled body was no longer hers, and how he menaced it no longer mattered, for she had departed that flesh. It no longer mattered if he raped the slack mouth, licked the teeth, now simply bone. It did not matter if he hacked the body apart with axes and knives, if he sucked out the stagnant blood, if he renamed and rearranged her limbs like sticks of wood. It did not matter if he ejaculated on what had been her body or inside what had been her body. That body was not her body anymore. Cindy was gone. They had lost her, and now she was ours. Now she was part of the morning fog.

On a Wednesday Night

Matthew Mackey

I saw on the news, our first
home suddenly caught fire.
There was nothing anybody
could do. The fire spread
from the bedroom of two
lovers, so they said. I want to
say that their bodies were like
flames, one circling the other.
I want to say so many things.

A fox finds a way into the
house through a broken
window. Maybe two foxes.
Maybe two lovers look into
a broken mirror. Either
way, there is so much red.

The water lilies were blooming in full
revelry. We know that now. Perhaps,
now, we even know how to say it.

So much at the

Jana Mackin

whim of baby talk: The lost ones led by aps to the gas chambers, singing hosannas for holographic messiahs touting turn the other cheek. I never meant to live this long; a kleptomaniac stealing images from the museum of meaning in ruins after the blitzkrieg of the media wars. I sit in this transit lounge, waiting for a gesture of insignificance. My future is predicated by sticking pins into the voodoo dolls of the Never Never. Make no mistake this is not the Never Never land of Peter Pan but instead the sanctuary where glucose depressed drunks come to worship. This is the land of dead fighter pilots buried upside down in front of the porno theater where Richard Brautigan liked to spend Christmas.

The Script

Jana Mackin

Much as the stars align with Touchdown Jesus limping across the Bridge of Sighs, a sandwich man advertises whiskey specials in front of Jim's Alibi Bar. In front of a black-wreathed door, he paces barefoot on a hot sidewalk, triggering screaming motion detectors. His labored breathing is a footnote. On bad days, the widow crosses the street into the air-conditioned haze. For a moment, heads turn as synchronized swimmers in a drowning pool then return to the bartender pouring long shots in honor of Jim's alibi. Behind the cash register, a plaque commemorates Jim's happy hour carrier landings on the bar. People still whisper about how she raked her face into petals of skin at the funeral. Once she drank champagne but now she tosses back Bloody Marys. Her scars are still visible through a black veil and she can't remember when she last received flowers. This is not the script I would have imagined.

Leaves

Whitney Mackman

This hole in my heart is in the shape of you.
—Jeanette Winterson

This old woman, she comes out
to perfect her lawn every morning.
The leaves always sprinkled over
the pruned patch: little green heaven.

She'll rake, bag what's piled, rest—
always wearing a floral shirt,
switching between the same few.

Sometimes I pass by,
look towards Leda Street
as if I didn't know
she'd be there.
Still there, raking.

Too old to be so stubborn
in this weather. Surely
too old to be fighting
an unstoppable force.

I saw her before Hurricane Isaac.
She'd stepped up her game:
hunched over broad shoulders,
took long strokes, gathered leaves
at her feet in a hurry.

Her house wears weathered yellow
adobe, sits by St. Louis #3. I run
there by the graves most afternoons.

Once, I ran out of love
for a woman I wanted
and now I'm the one searching.

A woman, to whom I once said,
"I wonder what raking
helps her forget."

Trigger

Whitney Mackman

Each weekend I fear
what Mother always warns.
No beer cracked, no shot swallowed
without hearing her voice:

It only takes one to trigger the gene

that convinced my cousin
it'd be beneficial for business
to mix cocktails and landscaping,
before he sawed himself off his branch.

It only takes one to trigger

the gene I joke about in bars,
deny in the liquor aisle,
fear at the doctor's office,
and swear could never happen to me.

It only takes one

gene lurking, locked inside DNA,
triggered by tomfoolery, chased with whiskey,
waiting to make me stubborn and sloppy,
waiting to tear my family apart.

It only takes

one too many to unlock decades of drunk
cousins, drowned livers, stalled hearts.
One too many till I slip and fall,
and hang myself from the family tree.

On a Wednesday Night

j.s. makkos

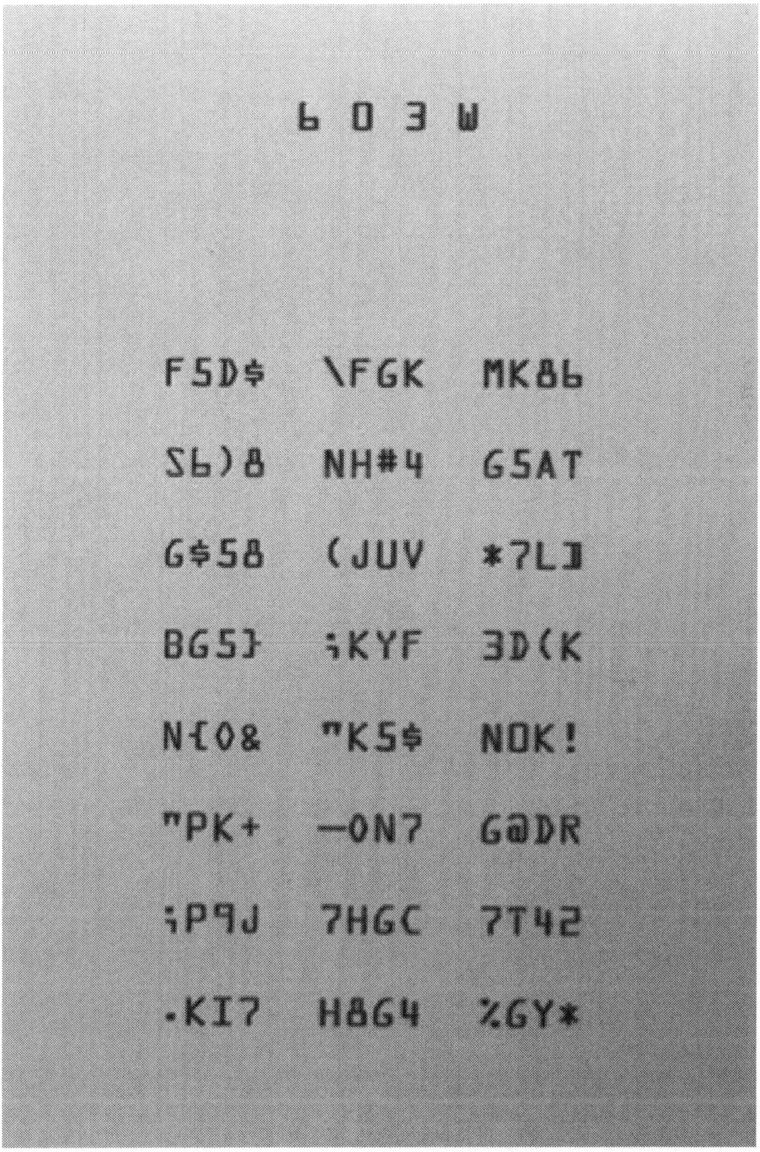

j.s. makkos

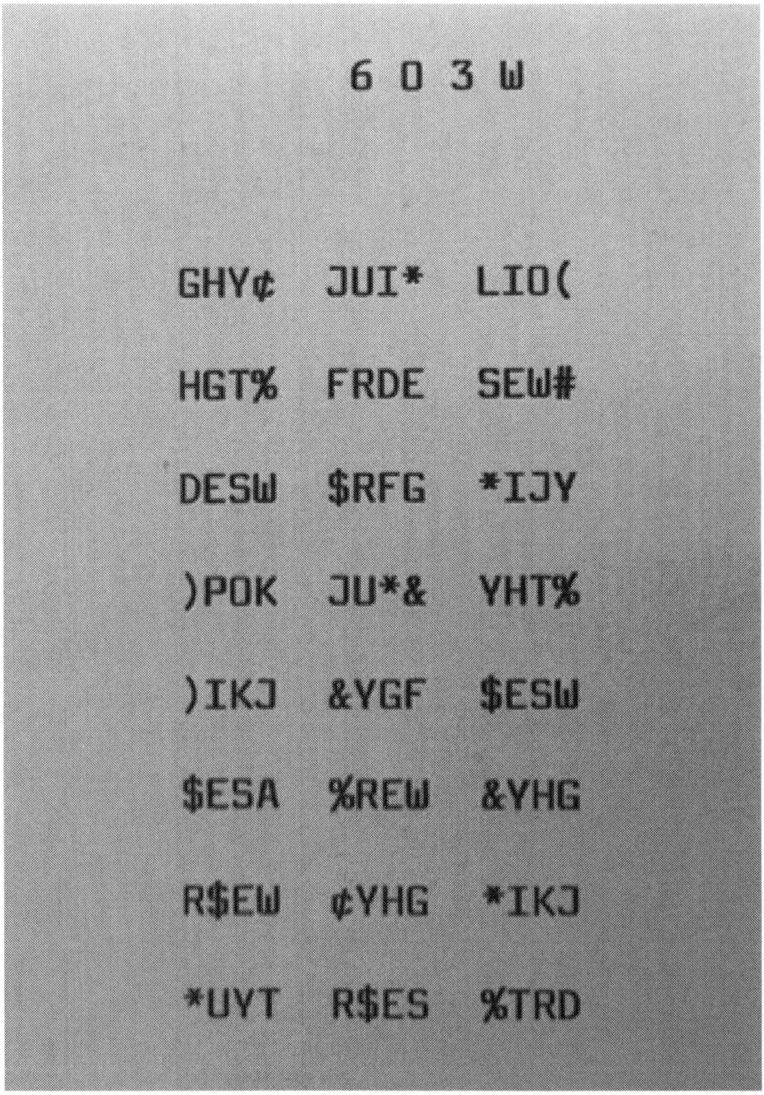

6 0 3 W

GHY¢ JUI* LIO(

HGT% FRDE SEW#

DESW $RFG *IJY

)POK JU*& YHT%

)IKJ &YGF $ESW

$ESA %REW &YHG

R$EW ¢YHG *IKJ

*UYT R$ES %TRD

On a Wednesday Night

j.s. makkos

6 O 3 W

E$F& LO(* MH¢T

U&GF *(OL JUY%

LO)(MKJU &¢FR

DE$# @#SD %¢YH

I(*& HYTF FR$S

LP)O HBF% &YFD

FR$# HU*& KI(*

FR%$ O)(I JU&Y

Today I Threw Out Your Toothbrush

Jesse Manley

Now only two things of yours remain:

The stain on my sheets from that time
neither of us could wait

and your running shoes,
which maybe you'll return for
because they still have some miles left in them.

How I Once Saw

Jesse Manley

How I Once Saw a Praying Mantis Impale and Devour a Hummingbird While Hanging Inverted From a Twig Near a Honeysuckle Bush, Splashing Rivulets of Arterial Spray onto the Soft Yellow Blossoms, and How This Singular and Relatively Insignificant Event Came to Represent The Question of Theodicy for Me That Led Me to Doubt the Benevolence of God.

It was quick,
then it simmered.

Juanita

Dawn Manning

They say she spent her last moments kneeling—spine curved,
arms crossed over her chest, head bowed—an ideal posture
for the final blow. Ambassador to the gods, bred of royal blood

for one purpose: to die before puberty could take root, before
her breasts could stir desire, before Mount Ampato could smother the world
in ash. Footprints of DNA trail down the Andes—through Arequipa,

Panama, Korea, Taiwan—witness to how far her forebears roamed. Ice Maiden:
savior of them all. Dressed in crimson, drunk on *chicha*—a flawless
gift to the gods betrayed by the fractured skull, shattered eye socket,

loose braid dyed with hemorrhaged thoughts. It took a week or more
for her to freeze to the core, time enough for her organs to reshape
around her last supper. After six hundred years

she shook the mountain loose: an ancestor searching for descendants—scream
preserved in the shriveled flesh pulling at her jaw; her wide cheekbones
imprinted in the faces of girls lolling at bus stops, knitting alpaca hats.

Like all things Inca, they bent her under a Spanish name.
Put her on display within the sillar walls of the White City—
rolled her over, knees curled in prayer, hollow eyes cupping the stars.

Fables from the Petrified Forest

Dawn Manning

I: Here There Be Dinos

Like most little brothers, you dragged a brontosaurus
around by the neck, slept on sheets scattered
with dino silhouettes, turned green-eyed

over the diorama I sculpted with a play-doh stegosaurus
at the center. In the days between myth and science,
we walked the forest-turned-stone, the dinosaurs

we were told roamed here proved by the scaffolding
of a triceratops ruling over a clutch of eggs
next to the museum gift shop—a pale anorexic,

her ribs a cradle emptied of heart and lungs.
We filled the void with our own flutter and breath,
a lullaby language we made up.

A few years later you left me behind,
fluent in a croon I could only fake, your awed accent
hardened into fear over how such heft

could just disappear. Soon after, you hardly talked at all.
So I didn't tell you when they exiled the triceratops
to the basement archives, dino lore shriveled

into a factoid about ancient crocodiles,
who lurked here shedding teeth
the way their descendants shed tears.

II: Fossils Are Forever

When you die it will be like this:
at the last second, before your body stiffens,
you will crawl through a chink of light,
scrape the stone-sleep from your eyes.
But you're at home in this gallery of trees—
this logjam of conifers and ginkgoes
that dreamed themselves into rainbows.
And you know how it is with trees—

how it's only the bark and sappy underskins
that are alive the moment before they go under,
the drought-ringed cores of them long dead.
Even fresh-scraped beams in a new house

carry a grave two hundred years in the making. Your body
and mind are curio cabinets displaying the fossils
our ancestors left behind; and if I scrape
beneath the surface, I know what I'll find. The truth is,

the light's already traced prisms
through your porous bones. Soon,
it will crawl through the soil of you,
seek out a different seed to nurture.

III: The Proof is in the Light

In the quiet years, we stood in the desert of toppled rainbows—
striated trees sliced into even segments like giant jelly rolls.

It happened so slowly, the way you buried yourself alive,
injected mud into your veins to smother out the air,

bones growing eyes in the dark, letting the rock-dense minerals in.
The sky collapsed on a Wednesday, and we saw the myth

only abstract painters from Sedona see: bruised skies, purple sand,
and seven thunderbolts at once. I tried to capture the approaching storm

with my 110 camera, rain washing out the trail before us.
Lightning sunk its fangs into the desert, the only love strong enough

to carve your initials in this bark.

Burning the Bodies

Dawn Manning

Dark night gave me dark eyes,
yet I use them to search for light.
—Gu Cheng

Dawn unstitches dark sky from dark earth,
a wound healed and reopened each day.

I watch saffron monks on the other side of the valley,
as on so many other mornings, preparing the way for the dead;

and I know this about the face in the paper and nothing more:
it took more than two hands to fill that dumpster

with six thousand bodies, numbered fetuses small as peaches,
and the bruised baby girls a few months old,

the names of twenty-one of them recorded on medical bracelets
buoying tiny wrists down the river, snagging fish lines.

Somewhere, even this face has been called mother. But the language
hasn't kept up with the times. It resists the generic word

for *sister*, but always that insistence of *mèimei*, *jiějie*—younger sister,
older sister—as if the world of One-or-Two-Child families

does not really exist. I stand vigil with the monks, all of us
without children of our own, smoke and ash filling the valley,

fluttering into my eyes and mouth like moths. The burning
in my throat is somebody you could have loved.

I carry their darkness in me, use it to search for light.

This Wet City

Jim McCormick

Sweeping the shed out back
        four times in a day,
I know that summer is round
        in this wet city.
        The Roman Candy man
passes and rings the bell
        on his mule drawn cart.
Women with umbrellas
        cast silhouettes
        upon the weather-
boards of old white houses.
        Near here
a screen door claps with its frame
and pulls two ripples from the heat.

New Orleans (Song Lyric)

Jim McCormick

New Orleans, wait for me
I'll be home soon as I find my way
Raging river, all of me
Is in your sweet embrace

New Orleans, always there
When this world treats me unkind
Cover me with your prayers
God knows you have mine

    There've been times I've tried so hard
    To run away from who I really am
    And there you were deep in my heart
    The further I ran

New Orleans, close it down
When you're ready, on your own
Tell my friends I'm alright
I'll find my way home

TASTE

Jessica Morey-Collins

I.

Dead, I make a menace
of a ghost—I am
the unruly host

of bees. We settle
to our knees, each
other an altar, petaled eyes

and marigold wings;
our disavowment of the finer things
corsets me. Here

it is not easy to breathe.
Anchored into haunted spaces

the Earth is a napkin, permeated
with grease from my fingers,

a photo I see when my eyes
close.

II.

Ants carry the bodies of their brethren
over bending grass blades;
sun creates shade.

I'd rather you didn't
say my name, speak mortar to seal
a foundation for blame.

You would have me as a womb,
as an empty baby cage, but I swallowed the bird
that had your face.

SUPPOSE LONELINESS

Jessica Morey-Collins

> *What I've seen, I've seen because I wanted to believe. If you look too hard you can go mad, but if you continue to look, you become liberated, you become awake.*
>
> —Fox Mulder

After the plane rattles its landing gear,
a man with a gleaming receding hairline
asks me to raise the plastic window-covering

so he won't be surprised when we touch down.
Pam—who has been softly scolding herself in the middle seat
—agrees that it's nice to anticipate

a landing. Suppose loneliness was a river
through the middle of America
in which we could plop boxes—

whole cartonfulls of opportune-meetings or fleeting affairs.
Suppose some bullrush baby floats
on its way to you, pinked cheeks just the color

of need. Pam is glad for me, on my way to visit a boyfriend,
& I can't muster the whatever to say we'll break up in 48 hours,
can't veer the toy-plane of my datable self
against the mountain. Two days 'til that plastic crack, when I'll stare

into your sheen & see only
my failings—my too-used toothbrush bristles
bent from months of brushing, the Cheeto-orange
finger marks I'll leave on your futon. A lover &

not a bullrush baby, no sky-worthy fuselage. Pam & the balding man
travel for work & wear wedding bands. They speak of home
and their throats are stovetops. They hold their phones

like wood axes, like whole worlds
pivot on their loved ones' words. Suppose loneliness

was a snowstorm, & the snow was TV static,
& that *I love you* that you said on accident during
an orgasm was the dark silhouette of a man
approaching through the flurry. Suppose a winter
plane crash. How bad I wanted to believe
I had been found. How the brain loves

to make meaning. Were loneliness a snowstorm, you'd be
an abandoned campsite. You'd be my crash through
scraggly woods, the fog twirling from my lungs.

DIRT HEART

Jessica Morey-Collins

after Darcie Dennigan

Bristly Dymphna, slipped from your unhinged father, your castle shrinks in its quills.
I rub eyes before your armaments. Your spires are filed
too sharply. My notes hold no
more acuity than your cedar scent.

Oh Damon, Dymphna's father, straddling a casket, a canyon, a sea—you won't
summon your dead wife from your daughter's body.
Just over the Celtic's whitecaps she waits: your run-off daughter in God's light,
  shedding coins.

The worst ghosts I've ever known are my own greedy fingers.

In the seventh century, as a seed at the center of the mountain, I could hear
the bell-call of Dymphna's pure heart to the headsick. Some asked her to dispel
  bog-thoughts,
some wanted the cobwebs mopped from their eyes & so cried out to her.

Few, if any, begged soup or shoe-leather. No, her virgin magic!
I listened—my brain-quiver ached for her cooling prayers.

My ears thrummed with dirt, rock & thicker than earthskin. I was only rumor & new
before my human birth. The earth. The dirty dirt. The spring-green of Dymphna
springing. I am un-rattled by the bell-call of her pure heart.

Did you feel the un-fucked mist of her twisting over the sea-top, the father-groom
looming his sword over the ocean? Her star-clean promise smelled like
lamplight in an old growth forest then. Death is never too soon among us,
said the forest. Return to that earth-dirt you came from, said the forest,
ask Dymphna's monkish escort how clammy the girl's hand felt as they fled.

I was potential and a vein of quartz, then. Just energy and a dust-dragged hem.
Mountain-swallowed, I was a mouth out of which a fawn could wobble,
little Dymphna, dainty fawn made of twigs and spit and shivers,
while your father coughed up his lost wife across the English Channel.

Pretty-stricken Christian, saint of quill-backed reputations quivering,
patron of the snot-sob ashamed in the shower, of the self-sliced skins,
if I ask you to tan my baby animal into leather, to beat me broader-chested,
I am asking to stay buried, next time—
I don't want to feel much more than dirt next time I'm born.

Her Solitaire

Jackson Moss

After Catullus

Ah my gem-eyed stay-at-home why not
let me dazzle you this afternoon?
Save the jewelry store for other days.
Skip the gym. Be entertained instead
by eleven consecutive fornifucations.
Send word my way as soon as you're alone.
Unlock your gate. Disarm your home alarm.
I've had my lunch and nap and now I'm up.
No diamond in your box is any harder.

Late Bloomer

Allyson Nobles

After the Hayley Gaberlavage painting

I

came to the party too late
carried my prepubescent bouquet to you
felt my red blossoms bruise, cheeky
    a rosy flush clearly seen
couldn't hide beneath fresh-pressed suit

stretched roots, reaching out for room
wilted only with your disapproval

I

left in the faceless crowd still
standing combed tight and slicked
won't last long in this heat
    reach out for your light anymore
become a bloom that won't ripen fast enough

have my bowl of fruit
have my eye on you

The Last Time

Allyson Nobles

After Aaron Baker

Enter: my sister's rapidly rising pulse,
irritating beep of the heart rate monitor, glare
of the sun beaming through the windows

the emergency room

where I am fourteen and feeling
gravity push against my spine, pressure
against my ear drums, beads of sweat

on the raised bed her body
shivers beneath white starched linens
awash and sterilized in the glaring hospital suite,

and I sit with my mom's self-help books
for coping with children who struggle with
drug addiction, but no chapter to help

the younger siblings left without understanding
of dirtied spoons, bloodied needles
scattered around
the shared upstairs bathroom

her heaving, deep and choked between breaths,
before she nods off to sleep

and I'm left with the lasting memory:

an empty plastic cup glittered with
red jiggly bits in and around it,

the wall splattered and sticky

just as when I once opened my bedroom door
    and first confused blood in the hall for cherry jello.

Michael Sleeps in White Sheets

Allyson Nobles

June 13, 2016

Last night I busted my knee on the roof of a Williamsburg apartment trying to see Brian Wilson perform *Pet Sounds* at Northside Festival. The wound dried up fine until I fell asleep, worried, and picked at it all night. I awoke this morning to Michael's peaceful face and saw that I had bled on his pristine sheets. I looked at my fingers and saw maroon under the nails. Iron. Tried to get some soda water to rub it away without waking him, but blood stained Michael's bed as last night's mass shooting will probably leave a mark on his identity. He sleeps peacefully just as he always has. My Michael for thirteen years. My Michael who came out to me in college. My Michael whose parents still don't know. I can try not to disturb him, to remove the stains, to let him sleep without worry in his innocence. But he'll wake up eventually like we all will have to.

As We Strolled Along On Canal Street

Adam Peltz

and a man with one leg purged
bright green over the side
of his VA-issued electric chair
and a sparrow beaked for food bits
making a song against the concrete
and the traffic flew around us
disengaged and honking toward the murky
river's edge, a red streetcar rolled by;
the Girls waved to the dark driver
hidden behind his mirrored shades
and mouthing a toothpick,
most of the riders seemed in a daze,
the morning sun struck and lighted the rails
and the faceless driver rang the bell.

Hangover

Adam Peltz

at dawn a silver-blue star unzipped
a part of the sky but to its own demise
over Franklin Avenue. The sun tripped
an unseen switch, turning the day on,
so the freight train screamed, the parrots spoke,
a man walked a little dog while another
stumbled by and smoked, a thin cloud
left behind. I dug for significance, trying
as the early bird. The choir of high-wire swallows
took the act: *This is the time to be alive,*
they chatted. A squirrel sniffed the line, tentative
to the crossing then went along anyway
as that is what it is meant to do.

In Memory of a Boy We Never Knew

Adam Peltz

beneath a silver Summer moon-wall
of light, the young fisherman might have picked
through his new tackle box before taking
the August dive into the shallows,
his neck cracking to one side as it struck
through the mush, finding the hard bottom.
Maybe his reflection had already looked dead to him,
his round face in the murky water
like a carp floating on its gray side. How peculiar
that as kids we padded along the splintering dock
in his final footsteps, staring over the edge
as in a fable, our own unfamiliar
faces not unlike his, hungering.

Grasshopper, plane

Ann Plicque

A slim, neon-green grasshopper
clings to the airplane window
with tiny, tarsal claws and arolium.
Its hair-thin antennae bend gracefully
in the hot, tarmac breeze.

It roams the compact oval casually,
settles near a bubble of dew
rolled down the glass,
leaves brilliant water traces
backlit by a rising sun,
stirs the bulb of water;
lifts it to motile, labial palps to sip,
moves slow, leisurely,
like a ballet dancer
making *rond de jambes.*

With delicate steps it covers the field
of magically-magnetic, slick glass,
until the jet rolls down the runway,
gains momentum, speed,
blows the casual drinker off.

We push into
our momentary
sip of sky.

Slow Blue

Ann Plicque

for Bee, February 2016

Waterfall—
creamy, foam torrents—
lick the back
of his neck;
spits of it meld
with salty sweat
from the long climb.

He closes his eyes:
the sound and wet
cocoon him
drown the sky,
drag him down
to the pool bottom
where he drifts—
arms, legs splayed,
in a cool, indigo womb,
to the beat of his own
slow, blue heart.

Marie and 94

Ann Plicque

for Marie Plicque Domingue

Demented, diapered,
Marie remains pleasant,
as she's always been:
Smiles, blanket-swaddled
on her front porch rocker.
Says, "I *love* to sit in the sun,"
with palpable joy,
closes deepset eyes,
hair swirled
around her head
in cotton wisps,
body barely
bantamweight,
nut-brown skin
paper thin.

She's mostly silent,
offers "Yes,"
to most questions:
Seldom knows.
Can't recall.

"I'll be a good girl!"
she cried out, once,
eyes stretched wide
in a waking dream—
like a child who'd transgressed.

Father's older sister,
my last tie to him,
dies in increments.
A hard pill.

Pre-Depression tales
dad didn't know;
snapshots of black lives
in Jim-Crow New Orleans;
tiny Davant; Point a la Hache;
her harsh, rough mother, my "Gram,"
the kind grandfather I never knew—
through her eyes,
die with her.

Sad as this is,
her skin feels warm
as I kiss her head
and hug her bony frame.
She beams,
thanks me
for passing by,
says "Good-bye," and
of all unimportant things,
remembers who I am,
and speaks my name.

In the *Jardín*

Sarah Rae

In the *Jardín,* the Mariachis sing.
Corn roasts on vendors' grills, scenting the air.
El niño tries to sell his Chiclets to the perfumed lady in the white lace shawl.

The newspaper man makes his final sale as he packs up the day's remaining issues:
El País, El Excélsior, The New York Times.
In the *Jardín*, the Mariachis sing.

Teenaged lovers entwine on wrought-iron benches;
nuns in brown and black habits pass them by.
El niño tries to sell his Chiclets to the black-stilettoed woman at the fountain, her breasts
spilling from her purple silk blouse as she reaches for her purse.

Shoe shiners at each corner buff and polish, polish and buff.
Children gaze at clown-dressed merchants with bright, elongated balloons.
In the *Jardín,* the Mariachis sing.

Mothers push crying babies in strollers.
Traditionally clothed women make their rounds with hand-embroidered wares.
El niño tries to sell his Chiclets to the retired American ex-pat in convertible khakis.

Lights illuminate the fountain's rainbowed colors, the buildings that surround.
Ice cream sellers scoop pistachio, vanilla, chocolate, hazelnut, strawberry, coconut.
In the *Jardín*, the Mariachis sing.
El niño tries to sell his Chiclets to the bluejeaned college students, their backpacks
dangling off their shoulders as they search their pockets for change.

Highway 61 at US 49

Sarah Rae

I went down to the crossroads, fell down on my knees. . .
—Robert Johnson

Blues highway runs
red, through cotton-flecked fields,

past the Heathman Plantation (established 1850),
First Eden Missionary Baptist Church;

rocky sand of the shoulders, eternally scorched,
spills into melted tar and black asphalt,

overtakes Double Quick Gas at Route 49,
the Guiding Light MB Baptist Church.

Heat vibrates silver;
a mirage of cars comes on—

past the Cozy Corner Café and Bar, where Bobby Williams
paints pictures of Blues artists on cinder block walls,
writes quotations from Martin and Malcolm X below tin roof rust.

The car radio preacher wails
about a wayward woman he knows;

she was spared from the *Devil's Inferno*
(and that *Heavy Metal Acid Rock),*
was saved by the *Sacred Blood of the Savior.*

Rubber skid marks fade,
orange clay of the earth burns—

Bobby tells how he went up to Chicago for a while,
tried to make it there, but missed it down here too much.

Steam pulsates the beat; rhythm shimmers
over open fields.

Rosy dirt gold sings
from under the blacktop—

the blood

Their Last Car

Sarah Rae

A mid-60s Chevy Impala—
white, used maybe,
paid for in cash.
Grandpa didn't use credit.

It had no air conditioning,
so when they came to get us
at the Greyhound Station,
corner of Busseron and Seventh,
on that sweltering August day,
all the windows were open.

Grandma sat behind Uncle Joe,
her black hair bobby pinned back.
Stray wisps plastered her temples;
only a strand or two of gray
peered through.

Late afternoon. Smell of road tar
and sweat. Cramped from sitting
in the bus, we piled our suitcases in.
My place, the middle hump in the back seat.
Grandma's apron squished cool
against my sticky thigh.

No "middle door pillars"
on those models, no metal frames
separating front glass panes from back.
Window spaces stretched long,
one on either side. Wet air gushed
wide, over all of us,
all at the same time.

Hail Mary At the Laundromat

Beverly Rainbolt

Fall 2006

As overfull with people as the plastic baskets, straw
baskets, duffel bags, mesh bags, black trash bags,
and grocery store paper bags that come
through the double glass doors are
with clothes   and everyone intent on getting out
the laundromat   it being a hot damned spot
on a brilliant fall afternoon in the broken town

when for seven seconds   we freeze
mid-chore   hold whatever piece
of cloth is   at that moment
going into/out of/onto the washer,
dryer, basket, folding table

we stop chugging coin-
machine-dispensed root beers and cheesy chips, hold wet
flannel shirts in mid-air, our blackened-for-eternity
roofers' t-shirts, our Western-trim shirts, our
button-down monogrammed franchise store shirts,
our blue jeans, work pants, khaki pants, cargo pants, our
Catholicschoolgirl skirts, and smelly diaper shirts,
our underwear

along the bank of gape-mouthed
dryer doors our hot towels, sheets, pajamas roll
'round to eleven o'clock and tumble out, our
socks mis-matching on the floor   while we
in the washateria hold our collective breaths, stop
speaking our four-or-five separating languages

to gaze upward to the ceiling-hung TV screens
—even the bottle-baby ceases his screams   serene
teetering on his Auntee's lean young hip

because Our Quarterback, with seven seconds
left, lets that hailmaryball loose and   hail mary   hail mary   hail
mary   the camera follows it for us down the field where
our hailmaryguy hail mary impossibly hail mary pops
up from the midst of three of those other
guys and pulls that big brown rosary bead ball
into his breast and lands his feet on endzone dirt

we mother-of-jesus explode: no way/did
you see that/did that just happen. . . talk about a Hail Mary . . .
return to our bending, sorting,
sheet-snapping, face-cloth-folding

—our clothes and linens fresher, cleaner,
brighter   and anything possible.

The Text Is Dead—Long Live the Text

Beverly Rainbolt

Words mill around in crowded chaos.
Language and *technology* square off, push up
Their sleeves and pace the boundaries of their turf.

Chicken and *Little* pair off, capitalize
on everyone's fears and run around yelling:
"The margins are falling! . . . margins are falling!"

Scrabble pieces clatter about the board
trying to land on the red Triple Word Score
spaces in bold effort to prove the edge worth more.

Magnetic Poetry Kits may have the idea,
words bonding in ways that cover
their backs, but leave their discourse

exposed to random acts of composition,
their meaning determined by how they fall.
If *sumptuous* lands next to *dead*

can the heart handle it—put it off
to chance, or to the symbolism of an
older order that could explain the way

things change so quickly.

Forest Park West

Beverly Rainbolt

my niece Janice and i had to ask Uncle Robert
for a blanket which he understanding fished
from the trunk off his Cadillac we wanted

to shroud the headstone of the gravesite-too-
ready so we could all more obviously not
notice five feet away the ground patient for my mother

while we buried Mammaw next to Pappaw on what
would have been their seventy-second Wedding
Anniversary September graveside service only

her friends all gone her large family gathered three sons
three daughters all seventeen grandkids she knew she had
but one. I almost didn't make it, too much a practice run

my mother was small and brave sitting straight
with pain we knew but didn't speak how soon
we would return to this same space of Earth/earth

then while my cousin prayed Mammaw down, the funeral director
up and died most of us saw the ambulance our gazes lost
(among the amens) across the oaktree/headstone field to the funeral

home office where he laid out on the floor (it's hard
not to laugh) while we respected the remains of my
father's mother her body now free to follow her mind

which had nineteen years wandered searching for my
Pappaw after he died and we living could put the blanket
back (quick don't look at the name it hides) into my uncle's trunk

and think of little else until February would be time to gather for
my mother was waning and i almost didn't make it.

Eidolon

Trisha Rezende

Here, at his feet, a suitcase full
of bullets rests, dangerous as a forest
of poplars (how they push
against each other).
The frontier will eat him
alive. And all he will eat are beans

and intent. When he lived with the swans
in the minds of men, often, he heard:
My neighbor has stolen my chickens.
Teach me to forgive him. My wife looks with longing
at the shopkeeper. Teach me to have faith
in her faithfulness. My father has passed. I have no tears.

Teach me to grieve. He crushed
marigolds into milk, wedged the pulp
between their toes, and became every lesson
they asked for. In this, he felt like a fire
that burns instead of a fire that doesn't.   Now,
he lives with rust and polaroids

and if he could cry, he would.   Instead,
from behind teeth worn low, he blasts out wishes
to, again, become an instrument of the everyday—a cup, a lamp, a
    coverlet,
but not a razor, though that is what now
might make of him. Once, *Teach me to shoot* made him a gun,
but his weight felt a burden, and his spit tasted too much

of iron. So, he became something else, something that carried
lessons like lead, something with eyes like deserts, something
to put down.

this poet at eighty nine

Trisha Rezende

once   the world and i were junkies   and behaved
like men about it   there was nothing we couldn't make
wet   not the one in the hand nor the two in the bush   we choked
graphite into all
                    the
                              white
                                        spaces   but then   or now
it couples with an other a youngster a beautiful monster born of ether
   and glass
and phlegm and beer mix   and dry   concrete on my tongue
and i have become desire's weakest cousin   thirst   an ocean
of pawn shops and barbed fences   un
comfortable with wrinkles like cuts that do not
bleed   the grass is greener
on the other side of me   mucus
runs from bodies the way butter runs
on fevered skin   stupidly
and without a plan   i had hoped i would always know
not enough of the world   instead   i know it all
is well that ends well

i am not the sun and you are not the sky

Trisha Rezende

imagine what the pigeon is coo ooing
to the plastic owl *you're a good listener thank you for spending time with me*
your wing span must be really wide you make this ledge feel like home
i try to not feel sorry for it why should i
it seems happy chatting away like a shy girl on a dating site no inhibitions
and who's to say that the plastic owl isn't capable of happiness after all
matter contains energy chemical bonds holding us together
when we don't have the sense to do so for ourselves it looks at peace up there
with that pigeon and that's closer than most people get to happiness sparkly
electrons and multiplying cells ain't got shit on that kind of peace i think
they're in love
but i'm not saying that i'm that pigeon i'm not nearly as chatty
or white and i'm a pretty discriminating eater nor are you
that plastic owl prince that he is he never encourages her to fly besides
we can be together in any other analogy maybe i'm the Coronary Artery
and you're the Heart or maybe i'm the Equatorial Current and you're the Atlantic
maybe i'm the One Star at which Castor and Pollux touch and you're the
Gemini maybe
that's too much pressure being contained and containing
let's be some things else
i will be the peacock plumage fanned wide and look upon you with my multitude
of eyes i contain all that contains me what a paradox and how fun to be complex
and you will be the rhino the plates of the earth shift in tandem with
yours building
and breaking continents you are strength and perseverance i am giddy
at the thought let us meet
under a Japanese maple growing in Quebec or under the rare Caribbean dogwood
and laugh at how it smells like coconuts and sex or inside the mouth of an
orchid or in
the ear of a god i'm looking at you Shiva hey what's up
or let's meet on the ledge of a building and make poems
and more sense than the pigeon and the plastic owl

Like a string of precious stones

Brenda Nettles Riojas

They shall not wither, my flowers,
they shall not cease, my songs.
—Nezalhualcoyotl (León-Portilla 1969-89)

Salve, the yield from blood and marrow,
inked on to the page—
truth, breath, the sacred in the now.

Even the Nahua kings paused
war for words,
flower and song,
in *xochital* in *cuicatl.*

Words like *jade, quetzal plumes*, and *flowers,*
salve, breath inked on to the page.
Each word tuned, cadenced to intoxicate,
to live beyond the now,
to pull colors from the sky and the ocean,
from the maize, the gold of the fields.

I see my song unfolding in a thousand

directions like a string of precious stones.

The wisteria beneath a Tex-Mex moon
intertwines its fragrance with the temporal,
clings to *terra firma,* seeks permanence
as my fingers sow new seeds,
space each word into meaning.

Floricanto. Salve, breath,
words poised to dance—the sacred in the now—
poetry.

Learning to speak the same language

Brenda Nettles Riojas

My first lesson at nine. My father tried
to teach me a third language, his cold war

curiosity, long before *glasnost*
and *perestroika*, long before we stopped

speaking the same language. I remember
a few words and phrases, try to learn again.

это моя книга [*eta moya caniga*]
This is my book.

The grammar books and records from childhood
dusty, brittle with age. French and Italian

found my attention. But Boris Pasternak
and Yevgeny Yevtushenko entice me

to return; lure me in with their words
in translation. One September I followed

Yevtushenko to New York, heard him recite
his verses. Later he posed for a picture,

his arm around me. Unable to get
any closer, I attempt to reclaim

a saint's Cyrillic script. The orchestrated
sounds resonate from childhood, from your

teaching me a new language. I try for
new ways to move my tongue, to understand

your polyglot ambitions. The learning
connected us, translated our distance.

Our own words inadequate for all we keep
silent now, I continue to seek understanding

in a foreign tongue, a *lingua franca.*

THE SPEAKER CAN'T BE IN THE POEM TODAY

Spencer Silverthorne

I am on the verge of watching a terrific blockbuster.

Direct your attention to the window. To some sinister expression
of light. To lyric exposing the wild interiors of the insipid. Bark
stripped from trunk, cast your eyes on the tender bleakness,
insufficient thing-hood.

You had me when you said I was prone to invasion. *I have fallen.*

I just made a sandwich because the bread looks better crumbed
and weaved into your beard. I just made a bird because your hand
looked like it needed a pecking.

I want to erase your hand. Lilies will have their way of rearing
their stinky corollas.
As if to beckon.

*I want you in my grasp because I am a low down body asleep under
a diseased palm tree.*

MOST ELIGIBLE BACHELOR: FRANK OCEAN

Spencer Silverthorne

I like watching sunrises
and I like watching you
with my friend who finds you cute.
Your crew and my crew probably overlap.
My friends talk loudly and flirt better
than my chirping, my flimsy repartee.
Mispronounce the champagne
and finally your manager would shuffle
you to the next guy. I can't be the first one.

I already know what friends say
behind my back. Hollywood
would not want my cadaver.
I want to test my heart
like a failed bomb.
It's why I prefer to stay back
by the shrubbery to line messy
swimming pools with empty bottles
that roll along the pavement.

He has ass, has drugs, has the car
he lifted from his dad. Los Angeles
is just like the movies but one thing
we have in common is that we shift
through sheen. The palms pink
way too easily to reach here.
Where I sell as much of my flimsy
demeanor and sell as much as I can
under the 10 until it rots and blows.

THE SPEAKER'S HISTORY OF KISSING

Spencer Silverthorne

Once I observed grandmother make that angel from block. Chip by chip, muscle emerged from coarse grey stone.

You were only dust in my eye, dust in my eye!

How did it feel? *S w e e p i n g.* Like the film I was born to die in.

This is why I need you here. Adaptation is difficult. Rodin, not pornographic television, enacted first desire. *A bloodless act could resemble tender little deaths.*

I could stare at marble for as long as our bodies rolled into rogue blocks. *Abandoned in yellow grass with morning light searing us stuck.*

Was my mouth created to be bludgeoned to blue? Won't you **big shot** me to oblivion?

Dust in my eye, dust in my eye. You took flight.

Once I observed grandmother make angel from block. *Was she making me you? Was she making you?* Chip by chip, you took flight.

And so let us decay in delight.

I want a gun. A gun's gun. Don't know anything about guns, but you know where to stick it. Bind my hands together. Take my pants. Keep gun in view. Press it against my lips. Apply it like red lipstick. Slap it against the temple until I bleed. Stick it in my mouth. Listen to steel fumbling against yours. ***TELL ME I'M YOUR DEATH WHORE.***

To feel like dying is something you and I must do to rehearse living.

Such sweetness from such silence.

An Expressionist Painting

Sophia Stone

In a tilted sepia room a woman labors
on a rumpled bed, legs pulled up, neck arched,
the sheet under her mound of green dress
smudged red. A braid unravels in her armpit,
her hands over her head grip the apron
of a blue table piled with folded laundry
in bright schematic designs like flags.
Her head turns toward the window or toward
the multi-colored chair where no one sits.
Through the open door orange stars fleck the night.

No, that's not a chair—it's an animal,
a pony, its back rounded into haunches
lime, lavender, rose chintz, its legs planted
firmly on the steep floor. And the woman
is looking at it, her hands, palm up, reaching
under a soft, uneven stack of dreams,
the blue ones draped over her fingers.
The dreams are marked with emblems
the pony has offered to interpret,
its pale green eyes turned shyly away.
It wants to tell her the umber streaks
are train tracks licked out toward the sky's edge,
their loads already borne away, the almond
rectangle an evening paper a woman reads
seated at the one lit window in a dark block,
and the wedge of gray a church carved
with wide-eyed saints, their fingers raised
in explanation of their visions. And more.

But she is not listening, her attention inward
on her own hard rhythms, although,
if she could speak, she would tell the pony
how grateful she is for its small body's
improbable colors. By the empty doorway
to this borrowed room, they are language enough.

Leaving a Freshman at College

Sophia Stone

Those cautious, territorial people pushing
through the door after us, haven't been here
before, either. They approach the way we did,
bearing their trays before them like the facts
of their lives, or a god's offering—coffee, bread.
Clan by clan they aim for the hobbled tables,
scrape back chairs, fold, encircle themselves
inside the steps and posts that mark the claim
Au Bon Pain has staked in the public way.
Most try to set their backs to the bloom of the sun.

A few graduate students, settled among
their friends, laugh, lounge together in the shade.
But not our rounds of strangers. Knee to knee,
shaping our loss with inattention, we fuss
over napkins, food—the hub of our old, worn wheel—
or stare out at the bright sidewalk; or else
we advise, leaning forward to tell, over
the traffic, everything already said
in the car, the plane, to the half-listener who sits
mute in every circle, letting us go.

I do not want the coffee after all.
We leave our cardboard cups and stand under
the clock in Harvard Square where years ago,
after four years, afraid of what came next,
I failed to make even one clean goodbye.
You bend over me like an uncle, your face
already turned toward the college gate.
And I can only tell you I am amazed
how things turned out—but I mean for me, not you.

Flying

Sophia Stone

In the early 'fifties, when his father died
And he was still in college, Charles quit writing.
He showed me his final poem: "I turn my head
And half expect to see my father's hand
Point straight again past Montauk Light.
The wind has maddened these Atlantic swells
Til time itself stops dead." Charles graduated,
Joined the army, then the CIA,
Operated in Cyprus, had a well-
Publicized and turbulent affair
With the crockery-throwing, alcoholic wife
Of his superior and got sent home.
By the time we met in Washington, he'd become
Truly anonymous: all his reports
For the Far East Desk were edited for style
By an endless round of faceless other spies
With no respect for decent prose, he said.

Passing Leonidas Street, after thirty years,
In New Orleans, I still think of Leonidas
And the hoplites, outnumbered, standing fast in the narrow
Pass at Thermopylae, and of pigeons escaping
The pigeon house. Charles read me *Imitations.*
I remember him jittering in the bathroom doorway,
Allowing just his book to flap across
The threshold toward the lit mirror where I sketched
My face in a dust of smudged pastel. That was
My art school year. I was twenty-one. Later,
At the Jockey Club, waiting for *les escargots,*
We gossiped about Robert Lowell. Charles called him "Cal."

Charlie, I saw you crying like a drunk
On the tarmac through my double plexiglas
As I lifted off our common ground for good.

I have the book, inscribed in your cramped print
"With infinite regret." The wedding gift
You gave us, balled in paper, "Icarus"
Stands poised on our table. His heavy wings still spread

Above the fretwork harness his father made.
His huge, indented eyes strain for the sea.
Perhaps, from another prison, Robert Lowell
Calls out, "Don't worry about the sun!" He waits
For someone else's hand to wave him on.

Palo Alto

Kat Stromquist

> *The thinking behind it is often obsessive and then impulsive; a kid can be ruminating about the train for a long time and then one night something ordinary—a botched quiz, a breakup—leads him or her to the tracks.*

i.

Sufficient anxiety is its own
persistent meditative state.

The years between 13 and 17
were the time I felt most alive,
mostly because I felt flayed.

Yesterday I had an argument
in a swimming pool about suicide:
whether it can be a rational option
or if it, itself, indicates illness.

Soccer practice, Spanish homework,
ACT prep, school play, cheerleading,
debate team, French club, model
U.N., driver's ed, maybe three AP
courses is too many but it can't hurt.

No, it can't hurt.

ii.

Buddhism urges us not to cling
to emotions, to drift on them like waves.

Many years later I remember adolescence
in flashes, the strobe of memory
like a drug experience.

I told my friend that another's suffering
is unknowable, and it is perhaps unkind
to force longevity
on another person, for our own sake.

The student waits for the letterhead
notice. The girl sends a pixelated photo
of her breasts. Disciplinary action
is its own failure to acknowledge
the ephemeral.

Everything's temporary, if you can wait.

iii.

It's the animals who live
in the eternal, spiritual present.

A photo of me at 16 shows big doe eyes,
shrunken breasts, a clavicle's protrusion.
Then a smile meant to look wicked.

My friend argues that depression
is almost always treatable
with the appropriate medication,
with timely intervention.

The fluttering heartbeat resembles
a deer's. A head swivels,
rapid respiration, the clanging
sound of the tracks like the sound
of the mind's panic distilled.

Then the train's gold dumb eye bearing down.

Crow in Snow

Diane Vance

Drowning in snow my yard is full:
no fish pond, no bush, no small chair, just wind
and drift. Bright sun a harsh illuminant
on a canvas now vivid and blank.

Crow wings cast a stark shadow gliding
across to land on snow. A black stain,
seeping slowly, a bird that talks sharp
and bright. Unfolding its wings as if

to ask, "How about this suit, not a bad
look?" It knows I watch as it struts and picks
through drifts for bits, hungry, tumbling
across this snowy land; a funny bird.

And now a jig prior to flight. Don't go,
don't go. I want for it to land, to fill
my salty hands. Rising crow at cocktail
hour summoning rumors of human

capacity, joy in climbing high
or making clumsy words out loud at last
a dispatch to this sad diaspora
of torn and wound-bound folk. Brain paths worn

by painful acts forgotten and now crow
glinting off window–crow mirror. A crow's
work to laugh away in flight and its sound
is a call that stays beyond its vision.

Sundown and moon up snow light lifts this room
to think of crow in cold dark not minding
an iota this snow that traps us, binds us
to land and all this crystal-lit longing.

Covered in Blooms

Diane Vance

Then let us speak of flowers if we must
disguise our hearts in pretty metaphors
that cloak all hurt and harm in blooms:
kaleidoscopic whorls and petals housed
in midsummer's abundance.
And who could not notice the breadth of this
garden, intoxicating nightly with scents
of earth and flowers engorged and sticky sweet:
perfuming the thickened summer air. Shall we
meet here where goldfinches color the
afternoon like fireflies enchant each summer
evening I come out here to think of us?
What is the meaning of these flowers? Is it
hope, this longing down my body where once
your tongue explored and my hands held your hair
so soft, or is it grief because I'm certain
we'll not find ourselves there again. Instead
I watch the flowers: hibiscus a needy
scarlet mouth that cries for hummingbirds
to notice; hydrangea mock me with abundance
for ever believing love would not change or choke
on disappointment—a thousand accusations
of what I did or did not do. Honeysuckle
vines planted first to sweeten the breeze but now
threatening to suffocate everything
in its path. We will wax nostalgic through another
summer in the garden saying *roses* instead of
I am ashamed, saying *wild violet* instead of
broken hearted, saying *bee balm* not
I no longer believe your words, saying
moon flowers rather than *I want to leave.*

Mockingbird Moon

Diane Vance

How do you sleep when the house is drenched
in this moonlight that filters through skylights
and shines on the stairway you will not climb

to her? Every night she counts each lonely
wooden step as she goes slow, like a child
punished and sent to her room to think on

it. Outside night birds call oblivious
to the blue sleepless hours; they trill
as moonlight saturates this darkness

and casts the trees. Shadow birds sing from
the walls of the night garden. It could be
her childhood, sticky humid summer,

fresh washed and thrilling in thin pajamas,
honeysuckled scent of evening drifts
through bedroom screens where she scanned clouds

for angel shapes and waited for the worst
of it: his shadow's approach in the silvered
moonglow. Efficiently she met his needs

and left herself alone with him. She could not
say where she traveled then, somewhere deeply
sad, where the catechisms of the weak

are learned by harsh repetition. The mocking
bird warbles and chirps—farther the train whistle blows.
She has known these sounds a lifetime spent

in small lonesome rooms learning what gives
comfort enough to last another night,
but not this light that haunts her with its shine.

Oh how do you sleep when the moon floods through,
and a night bird calls without ceasing:

How can you rest?

Bat

Lauren Walter

Insects I'd never killed
and gaps I'd never caulked
surely lured it to my home,

that bat. Between the carved pumpkins
and Mars bars, it swooped.
My clean cry tore in

half my laugh, my white-pursed lips.
What if I didn't know
how to say no? A wing

skimmed my cheek,
I smelled mango
on its breath. Bound

by a string of lights, still
I couldn't hide
how alone I was

every midnight, bare
feet tucked close
by the couch cushions.

Should've nabbed it, chunked it
with the red apples,
then candied the pieces.

Or should I have apologized
for turning it away
without sharing my own

goodies? How could I?
Out the front door, finally
he fled, a green glint in his eyes

that could have been my street sign.
And yes, he could call back,
but would I hear him coming?

Love Poem

Lauren Walter

Watch for distrust.
Watch for a garage door, slowly closing. Both bodies turned on.
Where is comfort there is complacency. I know it to be true.
Rather, I know it by rote.
Your pupils, each like the black silhouette of the Moon
as it eclipses the Sun and draws me
to the radiant corona surrounding it, swell
—rather, subside.

I miss our raincoats in the closet, both billed hoods dripping.
Shoes, yours, piled onto mine.
Late at night, the smell of your breath mild as a banana's
when I roll over in the middle of a dream. You, asleep, beside me.
        How day breaks.

        The leaves aren't green, the dead air's not breathed.
You can break your *amygdala*—or *amygdule*—for all I care.

Please don't open that front door.
Don't taste that breeze.
        I want day to break.
Watch: you, a songbird, startled by its reflection.
You, singing another's song.
        Circling and circling and circling until it's time

Sugar Children

Lauren Walter

What happened to those faces we saw as kids?

Out in the woods
behind Grandpa's house we said
they floated, less faces than masks,
as hard and as white
as our missing teeth. They chilled us
colder than the autumn air, clung closer
than the firewood scent in the mittens
we pressed over our eyes, scrunched
to see and not to see
those spirits, those ghouls we knew
would pursue us, without their bodies,
from tree to tree. In silence they would turn us
into ticking wind-up toys, into tops!

We rushed back down the hill,
slipping over the dead
leaves past Papa's utility trailer
to the shining house where
our parents tucked us, syrupy
from warmth, in our pajamas.

But I never truly saw any of those faces
except our own, cousins, speckled pink
from the wind. I nearly could,
our stories clear as our pilgrimages
past the mulberries to the cooling tower,
the dirt-floor shack a mile west, or
the blue stars in the sky

those nights. Winter whistles.
The forest black now, I go inside alone,
recite from a household book:
Dutch elm, katsura, blue spruce,
the faces, all our faces, lost, loose.

Gillespie's Cheeks

Patricia A. Ward

I had to look hard because it seemed so absurd.
On the handlebar of a bright red bike, a blackbird
posed with a pink glob in his beak.

Proud head tilted, long dancer's neck curved,
he blew bubbles that bounced with rain slicked
sounds. Aware that I was listening, he eyed me for critique,

I praised his style and watched while he bopped.
The bebop he rendered from Gillespie's cheeks
proved he had skills beyond an amateur.

I promoted him to sky song ambassador,
asked him to poke out his broad chest
for an award and to gust a farewell encore.

I had to look hard because it seemed he took a bow.
But that would be absurd. A blackbird who
can sing and blow bounce bubbles with rhythmic chords.

Hush Child

Patricia A. Ward

run silent as deer
bend low like willow

they'll be ridin' soon
seeking through dark

into day to take you back bound.
Hush child run quiet

if you hear man or beast,
drop, hug the earth, she's mother

rockin' you through the storm.
You are freedom bound.

Morning Moods

Patricia A. Ward

At six o'clock while we waited
for coffee, you went somewhere
inside yourself visiting.

A heavy silence lingered until
hot rolls came to table. I broke one,
buttered both halves extending

a peace offering, for we'd argued
earlier. I was finished with it, but you
hold on to your hurt longer than I,
and you would not look at me.

When my fingers brushed your hand:
    a beer truck rumbled by, early delivery
    steaming coffee arrived, aromatic pleasure
    butterfly flutters beneath your lids, refreshed
    you returned.

The House My Father Took

Tara Waudby

It was not the first thing he took from her by force
when in an *Absolut* rage deep in the night, my father
became the third arm of Shiva, holding his own flame of
elimination. Outside, drops of spring thaw kept time

with Shiva's drum, a slight ripple of movement in a
frozen moment. My mother stood still in the doorway
while my father woke my infant sleep with a knife
to my throat. Only he dared jar the silence:
"If you don't, I will."

Perhaps her mind flashed back six months, when he lay
on the tracks of the metro and she stood above him,
her body heavy with me, wondering how to save him.
Maybe she wished she hadn't. The house he demanded

with such force stood in Sonoran sands. Slump blocked
with a carport and three small bedrooms. My father
still held the knife. Time expanded from Vishnu's belly
as he molded the world with his deep exhale. Perhaps

my mother wished this Hindu god to expel breath faster, inhale
this dream for another. As she moved pen across papers,
signing the house unto my father, he withdrew the knife,
leaving only the faintest imprint. Then, he held me close and sang.

Arab Exile from Al-Ramla, 1948

Tara Waudby

This is the place, you could say
to yourself. This is the house
with two histories. The house with
the lemon tree.
—Sandy Tolan, *The Lemon Tree*

I can still recall the rooms of our house
built by the men of our family,
the long corridors that form a square,
each wing housing a generation.

I can still recall the outdoor kitchen
where Mama and my aunties
spent hours cooking in brick ovens
under the shade of our date trees.

But it's the lemon tree I can still see.
Feel its fruit in my hand, wince
at the first drops of juice on my tongue—
bitter then sweet.

Each year it blossomed,
heavy with fruit. Its juice set aside
for hummus, tabouleh, tea.
Its flesh rendered for sweets and cakes.
Our goats fattened themselves on rinds.

Despite our exile, we hear reports
that our lemon tree still stands
gnarled and curled
older than my father
older than my father's father, even.

They tell stories now of how we fled.
Ours a city deserted,
doors left open to refugees
who moved in while fires still burned in our stoves.

They tell stories.
But I remember our fathers talking
underneath the lemon tree, choices
weighing heavy on their farmers' backs.

Our fathers waited for allied soldiers,
waited to negotiate peace,
waited for the firing to stop.
But they came
unexpected
upon our fathers
who sat in makeshift trenches,
shovels in hand.

When our city fell
they halved the country.
Still, it is *our* home. Still,
it is *our* lemon tree.

Be Prophecy

Clare Welsh

When strangers say, "you are
too much to trust,"
what they mean is

your eyes shine like teeth

so don't blink. Be
a staring prophecy.
Surpass that old
Delphic Oracle
who saw opals only
in the gaze of gyrating
women. Find the opals
buried under concrete,
the opals clutched
in the roots of palm trees
like candles jabbed between water
washed graves. Friend, these

instructions are as much for me
as they are for you. Ancient
minerals shoulder our highways.
Driving down the I-10 with hands
out the window, we paw at light
pollution, the city like Constantine's
opal crown. So what
if he's another
asshole in a fancy hat
trying to take our money?
We no longer get our news
from the Internet, we no longer
know which Emperors to hate.
The suburbs are fossils, their ribs
grid the wetlands. We step

from the car, place palms
to soil. Sinking in ferns
and petrified wood, we dig
through the smell of wet fur,
extract cataracts, milk
stones, find in each
other oracles.

Nearing Extinction

Clare Welsh

When it gets humid,
I bend my limbs around cold
boulders, the molars
spat out by ancient glaciers.

Geologic time
is not romantic, but we
will still die in it,
soft spines fossilized like ferns.

Before going out
to prowl and drink, I comb
the Pennsylvania
woods. I find ticks. Lyme Disease:

An atomic red
halo circling a raised scab.
Like people on earth,
bacteria fight to live. This

is adaptation.
This is persistent motion.
This is a body,
a planet raging away.

After the Apocalypse

Clare Welsh

I will smash berries
into your mouth.

The berries will
be half ice

and half berry
plucked from a bush

sprouting over deer bones.
You will taste the deer

in the red berries.
You will grow

wolf's fur, triangle ears.
Your flushed skin

will be the color
of fruit, of insides.

Chewing,
you might remember

the rip and grind of machines,
the thick gray hours

of your work, how you watched time
ooze on the highway,

the subway, the sloppy way
you initialed all

paper. It will be too cold
to be romantic

about the earth. We will snap
meat from twigs, the dead

will shoot up through us.

Though We May Not Discuss

Kelcy Wilburn

white walls lit preparing the way for your home-
made love at twelve fifteen, your address
without twelve, add five and forty-three see

me looking at you and the perfect light angle
as you smear brown canyon over clean white nothing
as God did, and the screen of you in twenty years

washing your hands the same way but saying something
twenty years different, something inflated,
more meaning less, less of us, the cat gone

and everything with a hardness to it
like the canyon you paint over the white walls
in your new white home, the beginning

of us, the still soft shell that forms on skin,
tones shifting like canyon, grass cloth, and time,
though we may not discuss possibilities nor angles

nor the sum of your face, curls, or curls of smoke
lifting from lips paying service to some future

Waking Danger

Kelcy Wilburn

Be wary of the UFOs, I say,
their brooding shapes and
hovering sadness, I
thought to warn you
of their swarming today

like jellyfish curtsying
and propelling

slowly with the low, deep hum
of a freight train, a tornado
so slow and low, I think
I hope I go fast, and then

you kiss me goodbye
you're gone

Death Aggrandizing

Kelcy Wilburn

For Jack Gilbert (February 18, 1925–November 13, 2012)

Less encumbered like a music stand with only one sheet of music, or is it unencumbered altogether as one sheet can't weigh enough to keep the wind from carrying, or is it aggrandizing, his death? Unencumbered, the mind now lost and gone forever, no longer muddled from the waves of dementia. Aggrandizing, death, makes Jack bigger, makes each limited word limitless because there will be no more, no more hearts exploding from new poems, new words on his pages, yet the scrawls still there, unpublished, ripe for study of the brain, its limitations. Today I want to do my job, make people feel something in the way Jack's somethings make people feel everything, hearts exploding one after the other like dominoes falling, children vomiting in a line. "How was school today?" I overhear, thinking Jack was school and school was sad. Unencumbered, his mind is now, no blood pumping through, those words trapped forever in the confines of a skull buried or burned. There can't be a book on aging when aging kills the writing, when all the wisdom there can't overpower—such cruel irony. These kids step off the bus free and tripping and unencumbered in a different way, not dead, newly not dead as their days numbered fall wider on the spectrum. And Jack, oh Jack, I'll find myself crawling on the floor searching for your hairs now, as Michiko's in reverse, Linda's in grieving. Your will to live while living keeps me encumbered. Death aggrandizing. Must we wait for death, which promises wealth to no one? Just the art, we say. It must be this way, we say. "I do not write funny poems," you say.

The Front Porch

Deborah Brink Wöhrmann

for Adelaide Gonzalez

Nothing stays the same though we don't know when
an earthquake will strike
mountain erupt or a boat
will go aground at Pier 1.
We don't know whose child will live past twenty
whose mother will die in childbirth
or before her children can know her well.
We don't know how our own serenity will be broken or
if we will again find ease.
And if we worry about these changes we miss the warm May breeze
last of tulips' crimson bloom
sounds of sisters' talk
as they cross from their front porch onto our street making plans
for their evening
as they did from that same front porch
more than fifty years ago
teens in a hurry
nails polished red
long before their own children
would snuggle tight
into their breasts or grandchildren
would reach out for their worn faces.
Someone other than me sat gazing through maple leaves
curious as her neighbors giggled into the warm spring air
an eager dog sprawled and waiting
for her next chance to leap and play
marking moments.

FACULTY POEMS

American Ghost

John Gery

Not quite so collapsible
as you may imagine, these bones
of the fundamental country,
they hold up loosely within
the spirit, the American ghost,

fit like an elegant shirt
around a clean, lapidary body
so you can see they are cut
from the same cloth, no things
without the ideas we call them by

when comes the time to bless
and eat: We ingest neatly
the white corn. We inhale
after that the air, and swallow-
ing whole hog what we have been

given, we stroll out into the open,
even if no one else notices us,
the field itself we are crossing
much like any other field, fallow
for yielding us its rich future

after a rest. And we are assured
by our very invisibility, pressed
deep into our flesh, of ourselves,
footloose and bravely unseen
yet thought of, all the same.

The Enemies of Leisure

John Gery

At Jackson Square last Saturday at noon
the enemies of leisure sat down on a park bench
to plot their strategy against my turgescent idleness.
One of them, the one with the green skin whose veins bulge
around his eyes, reached forward and down to pick up
pieces of stale bread I'd left for the pigeons
and the wood on the bench warped under the sweating thighs
of the rest of the enemies of leisure. I heard a butterfly
crying, or was it a disfigured moth? Another one,
the enemy of leisure with the red scrubbed hands,
lifted lint from the overcoat of a nearby sleeping vagrant
as I gathered in my newspapers and started to rise, and
sweeping the sidewalks with his yellowed eyes
the one with pimples called out. "Almost Sunday," he cried.

They know much better the label to put on a pretty day
than I do, the enemies of leisure. They work at it.
I am a small miracle and I know nothing.
I have nothing to do—but to some I am a giant
and last night the enemies of leisure, all seven of them,
marched in single file up the side of my bedpost, over
my feet, and across my legs, leaving tracks of purpose
deep in my blankets, burning the hair on my chest in their wake,
then chopping back my sideburns to bury land mines
under my temples. Today I tried memorizing Whitman,
"I lean and loafe at my ease, etc." and "As to you Death,
your bitter hug of mortality, it is idle to try to alarm me"
and so on but it was no defense and I am fading, I am fading.
The black-caped leader of the enemies of leisure scaled
my green schefflera to direct his attack from its leaves.
Like Tu Fu I drank wine from a white cup but it's no go.

On a Wednesday Night

I am losing my fortitude, I am asking you to visit me,
the enemies of leisure are shoveling the dust out
from underneath my slippers, the one in the brown 3-piece suit
is crawling up my arm now, making small entries on a clipboard,
his pencil is sharpened, his eraser has never been used.
His prognosis is grim. I repeat, I am dying, S.O.S.,
come to me quickly, you're my only chance, I will save for you
the tracks of purpose and the warm wine. Abandoning ship.
This may be the last letter you receive from me
that has no point to it.

From *A Pack of Lies*: Lie #4: That Frances Osgood Slept with E.A. Poe

John Gery

They say it isn't sex that you remember.
I disagree. To think of Edgar's frown
that night we lay in bed till after five
talking about the future as the ember
beneath the grate flickered, burning down
to nothing—never had I felt alive

like that, I thought, he so preoccupied,
imagining every variant of death
he could, and I determined to give birth
to one of our ideas before I died,
the "curse of poetry" our shibboleth.
But poetry does not disturb the earth:

I can't agree with all that talk of spirit
he made. It's opening my legs, I swear,
ever so slightly while he sucked my breast,
then took my thigh in his left hand to steer it
over his own, coming inside to bear
my hips on his hips, I remember best.
I wouldn't scribble this, were not my eyes
so bleary from the pills and tea, like blood
flushed through a drain, my nurse pours down my throat.
She blinds my body so my soul might rise
invisibly, like smoke above the flood
of longing that slaps against this burning boat,

but I am sinking faster than her hope.
I sense the swirling sea surround me. Hate
I couldn't call it, but despair's the thing
that slowly starts to tighten like a rope,
as fastened to the mainmast of my fate,
I feel its spar inside me still. And still I cling.

Stump

John Gery

A hollowed-out trunk in a field, a tree
I never knew—catalpa, maybe, or elm—
to us a shallow fort we soon outgrew,
it withstood a hard decade of winters.

Look at it now: fat stub, a small lump
stuck in my imagination, like a breadcrumb
brushed under table linen. Frost,
no doubt, had killed it, or who knows,

a rare pestilence of scarabs. Yet glued
still to the inside wall of my cranium
it remains somehow, faded, to be exhumed
like this, its jagged edges splintering

above that hide of snow we loved
to puncture with our boots, stumbling
into its core. And it has worn through
the years of my forgetting friends' names,

the total casualties of the Arab war: a
trace of nothing, a place where I scraped
my knee once, sat on its roots, and cried
(though who can recall what for).

Lag Time

John Gery

Forever in between
appointments I am missing and
the ones I'm waiting for—
too little read, too often seen,
without ideas or planned
unknowns—I linger by the kitchen door

fingering a small book's pages
as though I had an hour to kill
when I have murdered years
already, years, and latched in cages
the rabbits of my will
to run amuck, fearful of what appears

running amuck. I'm late,
as usual. My rabbits fidget,
like dancing drops of water
on a stove, and then evaporate:
no caterwauling, since it
would take all afternoon to reconnoiter,

but just the calm I crave
cut loose from assignation. Clear,
contained as well-wrought prose
yet fraught with ease, the thoughts I have,
loitering like this, never decompose,
suspended in a time that isn't here.

Spring Offensive

John Gery

So little cause for carolings...
—Thomas Hardy

The birds keep singing in the dark
as undeterred as Englishmen
in Africa; my neighbors quiet—
sound asleep—I lie here stark
and fast, near the millennium,

bewildered and as unconsoled
by all the things I thought I knew
as empires by their allies. Still,
this music fills my room, unspoiled
as though it were the one thing true
my country hasn't tried to kill

or bind into its vast regime.
If I, too, could only sing, instead
of tossing dumbly through the night—
anxious to exorcize this dream
and rest in peace in my own bed—
I might not dread the morning light,

dread finding out what new assault
was launched in darkness from the sky
against whomever's next in line
to be disposed of. So who's at fault,
then, these ecstatic birds, or I?
Cowering in my own design

of arrogance, hung up on the air,
I'm stuck, the victim of their song
(whether propaganda or prayer)
insisting nothing can go wrong,
and nothing I do can defy it.

Paratextual Saxophone

John Gery

for John Cooke (1946-2010)

He glides along the edges of that mel-
ody like rain skimming the window pane
outside my bedroom. You can almost smell
the gravity, slow, uneven, its main
distinguishing feature, heard close, the strain

of each drop swerving from, disintegrating,
still undetermined. Like wearing loose pants,
crossing a street, no hurry, imitating
the pace of lingering by a shop, to glance
at pretty women, feign insouciance—

then, *bam*, he slams the brakes on (so to speak):
Mouth withdrawn from reed, fingers splayed midair
a moment (*pause*), as silence starts to leak
in. Gaze at her,—or must he rush from here
to afterwards, to where there's no there there,

toward what he's carefully avoided up
till now, in orchestrating the divine:
a kiss, the drink of water interrup-
ting conversation, or trace of the line
her shoulder makes against a pillow, nine

more bars laconically stretched out to fourteen? Relax.
Inhale. Something of what you said just then,
when you mentioned . . . but what? Between the acts,
in a collision, sound before it's seen,
the warm rush you get stepping on a train,

before you finish, time to start again.

Who'd Notice?

John Gery

A butterfly dead, crushed, the usual
    in this impassive world:
Who'd notice, were it not for the perusal
    of hikers, or the girl

you thought you'd never mention again,
    the one who addled you,
though no one you know now knew her, and then
    long after you'd recovered, who

in a moment of weakness, called you
    just to ask how you were,
when the thing of things that mostly galled you
    was how you thought of her

as not so needy, not so cavalier,
    to test her power on you
(decrepit you, arrested like a deer
    caught in the headlights), though

you had to admit hearing her voice
    aroused in you a jet
of toxic juice enough to hoist
    as from a trebuchet

both of you in the air, down on that spike
    again when you first kissed,
or how she snared you in her netting like
    a lepidopterist?

The English Major

John Gery

I know now, finally, why I hate Harry.
It's not Harry. It's what Harry is not.
All my life I've been waiting,
imagining any minute how the thrill
I planned for when I turned fifteen
would erupt inside me, maybe
three pm on a Tuesday, ice cream, or
how that billboard along 95, the one
like T.J. Eckleberg that bugged me
for five or six years, then faded,
would flower, would bloom, zinnias.
Three kids later and I say, brightly,
Bring me pistachio!, as the kids
without me go off with Harry.

I can't make it another six months
this way, another six hours sometimes,
I think. I've read all my Emily Brontë
three or four times. I've sizzled
on a stick ever since high school.
Day by day, I discipline myself, even
think belts for Harry. He just smiles.
But good schools, taxes, and telephones
finally don't add up. Thomas Jefferson
himself doesn't add up, though I like
fiddling with garden tools and bassoons
and built us a brick wall in the yard.
I'd even guess Harry has it in him
to dazzle, but I'm now too restless
simply to be dazzled. I need blood.
I need the charge of the light brigade.

On the horizon north of us, visible
from our upstairs bathroom window
where I sometimes sit, I can watch
the colors of the leaves change. I can
almost make out the russet roof of
one small house, snug among the trees,
like a kitten sucking the hill's small rise.
I could walk there myself in half a day.
I could pass under the Route 269 bridge
where they dug out part of an old crag
for the cars to pass. Every summer
the green stirs my one hand to reach
like an infant, though my reaching
is anything but childlike, first up, up
and out. Then down, with my other hand
across my chest toward my shoulder.

I think of that road, right where at
the bottom of the hill on our, the south,
side, it curves by a long white barrier
with a sharp drop to the right. Below,
rains fills the stream to overflowing
quickly, like me. I love, I *swear* I do,
my children, their puckered mouths
and light thin hair, almost transparent
whenever it comes out in the brush.
But I need to go away to that house
and Harry is not there, to dip in and
touch that wet stream with my tongue,
my four fingers. I don't need anymore
just to be dazzled, nor to be drowned.
I need the emperor of ice cream.

Brown Pelican on Piling

John Gery

I can't stand how that other,
apparently just like me,
looks, hunched there, beak buried in
her breast, one *out* bent feather
breaking the contour, the sea
from which we both hurried, thin

from need of shrimp or seabass,
receded for now. At rest,
thinking how I'm not thinking,
not of her, not this impasse
in the aftermath, blessed
by the twilight sinking

before the dark conceals us,
jaw-heavy, I forfeit how,
usually, I'd from her perch
her stretched long leg rush and push
off. I'll let her go for now
to spare her the thing that hurts.

A Cutter's Sestina (Prom '95)

Carolyn Hembree

Fuck spring. Spring's a punk in rose
leather who sings
under lacy stars,
stars the night bruised around:
My knives / are sharper / than your / knives.
Na na nana na. / Here, amid my corsage of voices—

baby's breath, filler, wired voice
I'll call Boss Fleur (my rosiest,
my loudest)—I knife
bloom upon bloom I believed. In what? Unsung,
in ribbons already, I'm around
to, what, suffer girls this Phantasmaboria stars.

Strobed grunge and stars,
you pulsing through gaps in my stall, govern these voices.
Govern these slits. Oh, we should belt a round
so we never cry, we never stop crying, should rise
on tides dyeable heels bleed, should sing
our aerial arrival, waif dynasty on a knife

edge at the dance no one dances. With knives
for mirrors, those stomped-cold stars,
we color our lips like our songs
before bright heads loll and voices
disappear down school and wild-rose
wilderness corridors. When limos round

the terraced distance with backseat cardigans, their round
necks, may every spike heel conceal a flick knife
for pinned torsos, our *oh so much* cuffed blubber, to arouse.
Feeling is a lie the crepe stars
tell the falsie hills in a voice-over
for a song

never cut. Didn't I say I loved a gothic touch, a snuff song,
a grudge fuck? Just look around.
TO THE YEAR THAT AMAZED US ALL, a voice over
the system. Have it. Where are the knives?
Where are the woods? Where are the starlets
who play my ghost and cover my creeping flesh in roses?

The Book of Foundlings

Carolyn Hembree

among torn spirals
drawing faces

an only child
found in the woods

felt understories
of trees within

the book of foundlings
sewn by hand

prints of herds
grazing near trees

spiral buds
within felt close

other arboreal
voices bled through

a sheet of rain
trees within the book

of foundlings
cones open seed sleeves

pine hems
cursive root hairs

of siblings drawn
felt her script

illuminate the blows
colonies underline

trees shade
overheard dream

a croon among the stems
they are sewing her face now

found in the woods
light paged through

Some Measures

Carolyn Hembree

Set on my soul an everlasting head.
—Raleigh

Less of, less often I see you still, free head—
now gourd in wind, now bauble by crib light

the baby, arm through scalloped hole, feels for.
O figure of speechless. Rendered up. What's taken,

what's taken in—not my milk (she fasts), but your dirge
she heard through coral walls the noon I stood

and you were buried. When more waves were sent
through me, I kept spotting, watching *off-on*

cursors in womb-fields. She's rooting, my rootling,
this paper kirtle leaks, *fällt die schwere Erde*:

Father risen from cilia grass, gyral knolls,
cerebella shanty, she's latching on. What earth says

heart says—
Like this swain song fading, you love your grief.

[Those liked swan songs fade in.] You loved your grief
in love to shy behind some earworm—Monk,
Beefheart ... *River of Shit,* I'd bet, nights ER
docs were like, *Your wife's so strung out!* Out walking
the baby, I hear *Like a Blister in the Sun* and your heart
bursts, again, your chest is opened,
                                        then *EARIE*
engraved above your dates. By any other name
would smell!—We'd have yucked it up. I strut my stuff.

Glass—yes, chamber music the night they called
you twice to the nursery glass.
                                        My baby's crying—
soiled maybe. The damp. The dates. The shade. A palm
in each, I flap, *Mommy-Big-Hands!* She claps,
my glass. What's she to get used to. You'd call,
Your mother's starting to cry. Let me go on.

Your mother's starting to cry. Let me go on
with you, my lines, our steins, red pens in hand.
How is it, Dad? *Cut and bleeding, daughter.*
Your voice, the wisdom you'd give by rote—Rilke,
gospels, one-liners, that gun poem, the one
you said kept you from killing yourself—now gone
or going. We'd go on until Mother's, slipping
into her cool bath, her baby voice, *Earle.*   *Yes, Baby.*

Here, dogs pace my side-hall in this seasonless,
sinking hole. From a window, I bid the neighbor's
plum whose blushing fleshes the frame
                                                            Manlier flower
                        Your head at the glass   Numinous bloom
Bloomed inscape. You knew I'd be changed, yet. Still, it's
almost as if I'll make my religion out of anger.

As if you'd made a religion out of anger,
I unfurled the way a hem of blood through water would
that night they called you twice, first for some boy
—oops, your "baby" still labored!—then *moi*. Aloof,
a Solomon before the divide, but you chose
no mother. I'd wrestle by rivers, pray from great
fish, fast in wilderness, be a son, sure.
Except when poems are towers I ascend, bored, robed
orb, folds falling behind me, until stairs drown
and days slope off, unseen—help, even the sky
don't hang with me. Be songs again that go:
My daughter is more than strings or wind, than pearls
emblazoned on my chest, this blowsy horizon.
Something to bow down to, I know, but what
of this world would you want for me, Father,
beyond beer gardens, a baby, these cut flowers?

Beyond the beer garden, *Baby!* this cut-flowers
lady waves, but like those insouciant weed-
trees waving behind our strolling, we are shades
amid the morass of our own making. We cut
through lots let go, flora gone florid—*[MOTHER
CELL]* again—shady banana trees, their mauve
schlongs adrip. Pass a Lady chapel. Into bell's
and horn's and baby's fugal ken. That school-

yard walk, you said *the president shot*, I saw
my tie-shoe, sidewalk gum become his collapsed
lung. We sigh.
The baby in its stroller. *The gun /
In its drawer.* I've blanked the rest, those lines you'd say
but never have the nerve to write. *[MISSED CALLS]*
Now, I am your gun poem. I won't be put down.

Now I am your gun poem, I won't be put down,
nymph by nymph, this May morning I hear your wife
fall: *Other worlds, dwell in me not drown! Daughter!*
What lurches whelms. She's sloppier than weather,
her red drapes parted: comely gap amid
such sulking gore. Her ways maybe but not
her part I've taken, and drawers of pills drown,
choric—*I keep you you keep me*—her snoring

wail, fingers that slip the porcelain lip. The time
you died, I was moved upon while halls were tongues
of fire that wandered me, my *[UN BORN, IT]* taken
for *[BURN UNIT*
                                        O]. (eyeslips)
                                                                        You'd read to me
some lines from what was open.   Dear, the born are falling.
Our chests shall open in the usual fashion.

The chest is opened in the usual fashion
and dissected as blood flows—*has flowed*—in

measures through you, measured, Father. To move
your mind to what's unfixed but shared is like

interrupting a dream that is a chambered vibe,

prepared to wipe away the walls their faunal
assemblage, floor its living blooms. *Die Blätter*

fallen, fallen wie von weit. There is a healing—
heal*ing,* how?— incision. I was outside

your door they would not let me through, epoch with moving

sheets on either side. Unremarkable and limited
to the trunk. Thy shoes thy belt thy cap—

I unscroll again these throwaway clothes I signed for.
Less of, less often I see you still, free head—

Writer's Retreat (Marginalia)

Bill Lavender

A shell to protect me
while I *work some things out.*

Parataxis: not a technique but
representation itself.

Ceiling fan turning
cross and gyre
in the dull evening light.

A simple single thread
that turns back on itself
again and again
and becomes a knot.

We write to make
the absent present
and vice versa.

A star sent out
that light we see tonight
a million years before humans existed
and after.

To turn over a new leaf.
To become a leaf
trembling in the wind.

A motor purring quietly outside
then pulling away. Distant voices.
Someone walking
on the wooden floor next door.

Whatever I say, invert.
Proscription is prescription.
Unity is division.
Etc.

I can say I but
if you'd rather
I can disappear:
it is an *aesthetic decision*.

The risk isn't discovering
you have nothing to say
but that you aren't there to say it.

The old wooden fence
weathered, green algae
starting up from the bottom.
When a gust hits
the pecan tree

nuts hit the tin roof hard.
I lie down stoned
and feel this as touch
as if I went all the way out.

The billionaire and the terrorist wake
every morning with the same
lust for revenge.

World is a rebus.
Picture yourself
here in this text.

Why if I am to be
reconciled with death
should it be in writing?
I built you;
can you contain me?
You, with your porch
and your garret,
your recesses and your mice.

Procedural writing,
writing according to rules,
feels like a narrowing down,
but taking decisions away
from the unconscious
actually widens the field.
Thus this narrow path.

Language 1:
The self alone with God
(or nothingness), space of prayer
from inner depths, the soul.
Language 2:
Self absolutely social,
intersubjective, populated
by others, pure mimicry,
automism.

That ache beyond wound
or hunger that resides at the center
of a perfect spring day.
If this suffering could be alleviated,
would the other kind also?

Beating time
to being.
For the time being
being.

That grand importance
of heritage, *blood*—
it is a text that teaches us this.

Lacan's single patient
was the culture that produced the holocaust.
If you don't get the *tone*, remember that.

Why the polemical
stand against division?
What is gained
from unity?

A storm, long anticipated
has arrived. Dead calm.
The eye of something.

As if the letters themselves
might vie with death, infect
it from the inside, kill it.

Is there anything more
hideous than a Hollywood smile?
And now it is every smile.

That playful, aggressive
spirit of youth, mock
combat of sports, evolving
finally into (a) real animosity or
(b) lifelong friendship.

The dream is a rebus.
Picture me there and
pay what you owe.

These delicate ways of wording
are of no benefit in speech.
Rhetoric is stand-in for the body.

The constrictor squeezes.
You breathe out.
It squeezes a little more.

Plato sees the psychology of the individual
reflected in the politics of the city.
Thus the *Symposium*, if you
haven't noticed, is an orgy.

If you look up at the tree
you will fear it falling
as indeed someday it will,
but lie down in its roots and arms.

Recording, in a manner of speaking,
the vast difference between the halting
oral presentation and the yet-to-come
fluidity of the writing.

People who are always
upbeat and happy
aren't.

Quintillian and Cicero imagine
they are prescribing strategies
for verbal combat
but in fact they chant
dreams in a trance
like the shamans of old.

Birds taking flight.
I flew into a tree.

As I wake from a nap my dream
hovers at arm's length, postage stamp
square of image and text, too far away
and poorly lit for these failing eyes to read.

"The measure of language is its use."
But "use" implies will, a speaker's mastery
(and speech of a Master)
as well as a further purpose.
What of language that erupts?
The slur, the slip, the swear?
What if language were not a thing we use
but a thing we are used by?
The measure of language is it's us.

To have an aesthetic is already an ideological decision.
There is no "right wing" art.
Even the work that attempted to be that
(Pound, Dalí, Marinetti) was ignored by the right
and then co-opted—in brackets, with redactions—
by the left.

Our critiques of the Other…
Hypocrite is not, etymologically,
hypo-critical, but an actor,
lines preordained,
not to be argued with
except by another actor.

Ant hive functioning as a single
organism or a school of fish
turning at the same moment…
but no animal is more fully
linked to the tribe,
no subject more intimately
intersubjective than the human.

No matter how I try to isolate
myself, there you are, looking
over my shoulder.

Would it be better, more *authentic*,
to make this appeal in speech
rather than writing? Speaking to you,
perhaps, or an imagined you.
Or speaking quietly to myself.
Or simply thinking.

The lush gardens of early summer.
That heavy, humid heat that weighs
on everything as it strives
to get out of the ground.

I keep forgetting that word "muscadine."

Who is a master of language?
It's like saying, "I can swim therefore
I am master of the ocean.
The waves move at my will."

Something you can bet on:
Whenever there is inexplicable
mischief—a lamp knocked over,
a hole in the screen, edged
with light gray fur—
a squirrel is involved.

"Stop," her voice
from next door, the tactile
pleasure of it, of being
familiar with it.

Is a *professional writer* one who
writes for money or
one who professes to?
For what will I exchange this?
What will you pay?

Could the prayer be made neither
in speech nor writing nor even language
but in some other signifying system?
Hieroglyphs, perhaps? Images, a rebus?
Or in music? Or perhaps

in money? A poem
in money.
The dove drops out of its nest
straight to the ground
where it flops, pitifully
with a broken wing.
But when I (9 years old)
get close enough to touch
it miraculously recovers and flies away.

If I point to the mirror on the wall
and say, "me," I speak truly.
And if I break out the mirror
and repeat the gesture to the empty frame
I again speak truly.
Where it was I must come to be.

Two electricians driving to a job
in the company van, listening to the radio.
All day they string wire through the bones
of a building while the current
of the culture courses through them.

A poet tells me:
"When I'm writing, I try not to read anyone else,
so as not to corrupt my point of view."
A novelist tells me:
"If I read for three hours, I feel guilty because
I think that's time I should have spent writing."
The MFA fantasy is the same
as the capitalist fantasy.

Idea for a drawing:
Skeleton with a pot belly.

meanings meet
in the hollow.

Poetry that ancient broken
pottery of sound.

The proper name alone
is enough to graft the child
onto the tree of language.
After that, all the
limbs of grammar follow.

Why are you in prison?
Because I committed a crime.
What crime did you commit?
The crime of performing an imprisonable act.

If you want to
speak truth
say you lie.

Discourse reverts
to incantation, last prayer
as the tiger bears down.

Duped by
duplicitous nature.

The woman walking in front of me turns
around, sensing my eyes on her.
We are all together, we
all *sense* together in the single
network of desire.

The fact that we can
ask the meaning of meaning
means there is none.

Tiny signs, least
movement of eye or lip,
smallest inflection of the shoulder,
signs as minuscule as letters
on a page.

My true
and irrevocable
solitude
in this matter.

Shell I've outgrown,
let some other
hermit camp here.

Canticle for Our Affair

Kay Murphy

The light, a convex mirror,
your round face fired in my hall
of familiars. Musk of your dog

after her fall into the river
still clings to the woven waves
of my black turtle neck.

We call it delta down here,
your voice the violet of sunset
pouring into the western sky.

We want to feast, fearless
as the gulls wheeling above us,
a flocked halo of feathery flaps.

How difficult it is to be fed
by wind under waterless clouds
a woman in sore need

laughing if we could call it that
pitched this way that way exposed
like sheets stripped for the next lover.

We catch what we still can
on the wing, rocks hidden below
water; we lick time into an arc,

tick in our wildness. The sun
snuffs out when you pull
the black sweater over my eyes.

My Mother Called Me

Kay Murphy

My mother had a dream in which I entered
her bedroom calling *Mom, Oh Mom* until
my voice pulled her from something…
inscrutable? *What*, she said and opened her eyes.
I simply answered, *The Lord is here,* as if someone
less important than a gentleman
caller without flowers had arrived.

Although she is nearly deaf, I only had to
say this awful thing about the Lord once.
What happened then, I asked
terrified to be the harbinger of my mother's death.

Nothing, she said, *I called because I want to know why*
you came back to see me so soon and why
you said what you said.
                                        No words of logic convince her
now it was a dream.
                                    That evening, after work,
my lover asked me if I had something
on my mind. *No, Why?,* I lied. *At 2 am*
you were not in the bed. I thought you might be
reading but no light was on.

I cannot explain this. I live 12 hours away
from my home town. I don't know the Lord
well enough to introduce him to my mother.
Now, what do I tell her?
Or should I leave that to the Lord?

Undiagnosed Villanelle

Kay Murphy

I lie half-crazed on a cement bed,
Temp 102. *I'm on a grave, a table?*
The nurses make their rounds in shoes of lead,

Rolling pcs, forms to sign, and my *one* med
Until the virus has a label.
I lie half-crazed on a cement bed.

I want to tell them that I feel code *red*
But words are coiled in my right lung, a taut cable.
The nurses make their rounds in shoes of lead.

Not like a plum but like an eggplant head
My vein is blown. I'm more unstable
As I lie half-crazed on a cement bed.

It baffles bio labs what bastard bugs have bred…
Shh! Those harsh sounds hurt my brain, and a babble
Of nurses make their rounds in shoes of lead.

I'll think up delirious sex scenes instead
While the cultures grow, while I am still able.
I lie half-crazed on a cement bed,
The nurses make their rounds in shoes of lead.

The Taking Back

Kay Murphy

for C

I still don't know where those keys went
I thought fell from my purse
onto the floor of Rolls N Bowls
where we slurped glass noodles,
or those tickets to Etta James
at the House of Blues (where we
then had to stand out on the street
under one umbrella), or those 3D glasses
that curved our limbs into rainbows
under the bedroom lamp, or that big yellow
cat we called Taxi that walked out on us.

And you? Where did you go while
I sat listening to all of your reasons
for leaving me, lying, saying we had
nothing in common, lying, saying
it had been over for a long time,
while I lie on the couch sobbing.
So sweetly then you came to me
and said you didn't mean it, you'd
take it back.   And where did that go?

White bird when you were with me I knew your name

Kay Murphy

White bird in my dream you wore a black mask and perched
in the hot pink crepe myrtle in the backyard
in the backyard I once owned with my lover
in the lover who lived with me by the bayou
in the not-blue bayou where I meditated every morning
in the mornings after we had made love
in the last days of forever before the dream

White bird whose bill is not black
whose bill is not grayish
whose bill is kumquat
whose bill is hooked
whose bill is a scythe
whose bill is a four-day moon in October
whose bill should be a dead giveaway

White bird studying the ground
like a scientist on the verge of a great discovery
like a monk in emptiness
like a mime whose livelihood depends on stillness
like a painting by Walter Anderson
like a hungry white bird

White bird whose legs are new bamboo
you are not a *Casmerodius albus* for your legs are not black
you are not an *Egretta thula* for your bill is not black
you are not a *Bubulcus ibis* for your bill is not short
you are not an *Eudocimus albus* for your face is not bare
you are not a *Calidris himantopus* for you are too far south

You came on the night of a death
not just any death
not a death that made the front page
not a death that was expected

not a death that was timely or natural
not a death you could say was entirely accidental
not a death everyone mourned but
not a death from which I will recover

White bird not in the bird book, how will I know you next time?

The Phenomenology of Blue (from "The Ascent of Joy")

Kay Murphy

There are connoisseurs of blue, just as there are connoisseurs of wine.
—Colette

Why is it madder blue's the one I long for
when my lover waves the paintbrush, baton like,
over the walls and asks, *Between these several*
mixed blue patches, which blend would you prefer
to stare at when you're writing? Trying to choose

sends me into a reverie of objects
that complicate both questions: bluebells bedded
along the galvanized hot tin shed; pecked out
eggshells of the robin's brood; lined up naked-
headed Jays on a Live Oak's limb who catch

tossed in-shell peanuts. Their glaucous fur and feathers
shedding from the bayou's toxic mercury.
Yet, they almost stand on tiptoe when they sing.
Sparrows splattering mulberry on sheets
that twist under the wisteria-stormed sky;

my periwinkle convertible belching
smoke along I-55. Then, two stillpoints:
a blue heron looking tranquil but alert;
peacock feathers dusty in a damson vase
from one of my dead friends.

I hate to see
a thing of beauty die—even the stinging
Portuguese Man-of-War, bane of the bather,
washed up on the beach by high tide one morning:
his twisted tentacles, his see-through azure
glob of body, inky tail strung out the length

of a human. That spiny top ridge edged
in pink the only flush. While the glutinous
near-fatal poison seeped into the sand and
we worried over who was stung, a bluefish,
voracious, migrating—or a barracuda,

fang-toothed—tore chunks of muscle from a boy's
right thigh not far from the beach house where I,
inside drawn shades, did not notice. But when I did,
the ocean, as far as I could see was venom,
glittering like what I knew was in my veins:

a noxious mixture of my father's truck oil
and my mother's Lethe *soup d'jour* so that I
can't remember that I've journeyed, but my lover
who told me when I cried out, startled, *It's just
a nightmare.* But I know it is that crazy blue.

Hometown

Kay Murphy

Good is what we can do with evil.
—J.V. Cunningham

The small son of a man my father worked
for passed him once without a glance, turned back
to stomp a lounging yellow cat, which jerked

a time or two. At 25, for crack,
he roped together newlyweds, then folded
their living bodies inside a burlap sack

he lit with kerosene. He swore, I'm told,
on *America's Most Wanted,* to kill
all the *sonzabitches* when he's paroled.

There is no doubt in my mind that he will,
and just as good a chance he'll prove he's framed.
A town like ours can never get its fill

of evil. Twelve bars, three steeples all the same,
town square where they auction hogs. It's so small
the auctioneer's the county judge. Our fame

spread to Chicago where gangs they call
Sicilian Serpents bought our Pizza Hut,
a Mafia front; the coroner invited all

his *nouveaux riche,* with their 14 carat
disco chains, to rape the dead; our mailman dealt
narcotics. More than once I fought

off the chiropractor, and neighbor, who felt
me up, as did my dad's best friend, who thought
because I was a female, *ergo* a slut.

The sheriff still pays a dollar for a cat pelt.

A Friend Congratulates Me on Getting Up

Kay Murphy

They do not break up their lines to weep.
—Yeats

The Dalai Lama, a man I emulate,
prays every morning for the Red Chinese,

who killed the lamas, sacked the monasteries,
desecrated sacred texts. So I meditated.

But I couldn't bring myself to pray.
I fed the cat, I gave the birds some treats.

I cut a credit card in half and called
my mother, who hoped her friend was voted in

as coroner, but hadn't heard the news.
I made some calls for her about some bills

she doesn't owe. Then Sister Mary Rose
from book club called, in panic. Her cancer's back,

left thigh. Bewildered, I asked, *But you believe*
in God. So why worry? She hung up on me.

Midafternoon I went to Hannah's and stripped
for my massage. My neck locked in a spasm,

my back a riverbed of rocky knots.
The music she had on was irritating—

I soon, though, recognized the Sanskrit,
a string of lapis syllables that heal,

the same discolored gem in Yeats' poem
carved into three monks ascending to their hermit

lodge for mournful song. They looked on
all the tragic scene. But once the music

drifted through the clouds, the dread
transfigured. Now, *if nothing drastic is done,*

we may find ourselves beyond thc tragic.

Waiting for That Dark Center

Kay Murphy

after Rilke

where procreation flares
at night, our best time together;

in morning after th767yse children went to school,
a steaming cup to my lips, the clock
knocking, restless, on the desk;

in the ER when all I could do was wait;

in meditation listening to Monk and Miles
Coltrane and Corea
no words between us.

In Greece, at Delphi, the Castilian Springs
had turned to dust
but the sea glittered sapphire;

velvet poppies spilled down between rocks.
I made a prayer that you
would never leave me.

My friends want to know where you are.
I tell them even when you do appear,
I am wasting my life.

On *El Día de Los Muertos* Neruda Speaks to Me

Kay Murphy

2 November 2003

To think, I almost missed the party because every day
is the Day of the Dead. I'm always in black, but this night

everyone is: the orphaned woman in a top hat and dustcoat,
a man in a black wedding gown, a beret pinned with a crucifix.

An altar sparkles with photos; the faint breath
of the posed flickers the candle light that stings their eyes.

Neruda's words are recited in English, Arabic, lispy Spanish.
The Flamenco dancers pound the earth to vibrate the dead

into dancing, pound until the small casket I saw in Nepal
needs only a lid and the boy's body, so like my son's.

The drummer's palms pound a wooden drum until the boy's
stiff young body is placed on the pyre, with his head to the east.

His mother screams for the third, ritualized time.
The Lama packs butter onto his soles and his eyelids, into

his ears, his mouth, his anus, so the *alma* when it is time,
can set forth only through the crown aperture. The flesh

burns for hours along with the pine casket splintered
under the juniper branches. But Neruda still has enough words.

I do not know the boy nor his mother unless they are me.
I speak to her in a language only she and I comprehend.

My son, who looks like he has been awakened from the dead,
enjoys this night. Why does it seem that the living suffer

more than the dead, yet the living want only to live?
After the music stops and the dancers bow, Neruda says,

through tongues of fire that lick the living like a dog a wound:
Hurl yourself into your grief like a dove, like snow on the dead.

Who, on this night, knows who are the living, who are the dead?

CONTRIBUTORS

GRADUATES

Nordette N. Adams (2016) grew up in New Orleans. Her poetry has appeared in *Rattle Magazine, Unlikely Stories IV, Quaint Magazine, About Place Journal,* and *Nasty Women Poets: An Unapologetic Anthology of Subversive Verse.* Her essays have been included or referenced in multiple books and journals and on websites such as *HuffPost, SheKnows, NOLA.com, Slate, Vox,* and the *Washington Post.* "Reports from the Laser Interferometer Gravitational-Wave Observatory" appeared in *About Place Journal,* Vol. IV, Issue I, 2016. "Sidebar While Making a Bucket List" appeared as "Scrawl" in *Unlikely Stories IV*, "Black Arts Matter" edition, 2016.

Mawiyah Kai EL-Jamah Bomani (2008) is a native New Orleanian Writer Spirit Woman OloriIfaniyi Wife Mama Red Rain Worshipper Spirit Walker Goopher Dust Weaver Wombniversal Healer Writer Diviner New Orleans HooDoo Diva. Her writings have appeared in *The Crab Orchard Review, Dark Eros, Catch The Fire, Freeform Magazine, Beyond The Frontier, Kente Cloth, Fertile Ground, Family Portraits, Chicken Bones: A Literary Journal, Survival Digest Quarterly, From A Bend In The River, Thicker Than Water, The House of Misfit's Guide to Spiritual Enlightenment, Essence Magazine, Keeping it Hushed: The Barbershop African American Hush Harbor Rhetoric, Looking for Soul, Black Poetry Music, The Louisiana Poetry Project and Women's Issues and Feminism in the 21st Century.* She is co-writer/director of the play Brown Blood Black Womb. She is also writer of the plays Spring Chicken, Crows Feet, Bourbon and Hair Anthem, and Spring Chicken which won playwright of the year in 2013. Mawiyah is an educator, Egun Medium, Priestess of OYA in the Yoruba system of spirituality where she is addressed divinely as Olori Iyanifa Aboyade Omobola Bomani. She is editor of *OyaN'Soro,* an explorative Ezine of Ifa understanding and Afrikan cultural identity and ideology. Mawiyah earned her bachelor's in Print-Journalism and English Literature from Southern University at New Orleans and a teaching certificate in Special Education from the University of New Orleans. Mawiyah currently lives, writes, and conducts Orisa rituals and root work in her home state of Louisiana.

She is often quoted as saying, *"If you wanna know where you going call yo ancestors, dial em up with your sanctified juju. The juju you was born with fore time knew your name."*

Jonathan Brown (2016) also holds a BA in Communication from the College of Charleston and an MA in Writing and Consciousness from New College of California. In 2013, he was awarded the John Woods Scholarship to study in Prague. His poems have been published in the *Worcester Review, The Nashville Review, Wordplaysound,* and *Indiefeed*: Performance Poetry. He won the 2010 and 2012 Tennessee Williams Literary Festival Poetry Slam in New Orleans. He's a nine-time finalist at the LEAF Poetry Slam and the 2006 Bay Area Slam Champion. He has been a member of five National Poetry Slam Teams. His focus now is hip hop. He's shared the stage with Milo, Sage Francis, Saul Williams, Sole, Sadistik, Weerd Science, Bluebird, and Blueprint. On the stage, Jonathan is a rhinoceros, trouncing around; on the page, he's an alchemist, transmuting vulnerability into a source of peace. He's a prism splitting light in all directions. Jonathan was a high school English teacher for eight years. Now he tours the country and rocks shows.

Joseph Buckley (2016) is an artist who takes residence in New Orleans.

Lauren Capone (2014) is a poet, baker, gardener, and Star Trek enthusiast who lives and writes in New Orleans. "Symmetry of a Purge" appeared in *Sundog Lit.*

Carrie Chappell (2013) is originally from Birmingham, Alabama. Her poetry has appeared in *Anastamos, Blue Mesa Review, CALA MITY, Cimarron Review, Cream City Review, FORTH Magazine, Harpur Palate, Juked, Pittsburgh Poetry Review*, and *The Volta*. Her reviews have appeared in *The Collagist, Diagram, FANZINE, The Iowa Review, Xavier Review*, and *Buried Letter Press*. Currently, she lives, writes, and teaches in Paris, France. "transcendental ethel" appeared in *Those That This*, July 2016.

Barbara Darcey (2004) left New Orleans for New England after Hurricane Katrina in August 2005. Four years later she returned to Covington, Louisiana, with her husband, children, and five pets. Her jobs in the last fifteen years include web content producer, Public Affairs and Marketing for a major rural medical center, as well as several years teaching at the high school and college level. She currently lives in Sarasota, Florida. She has completed a graphic novel and several small collections of poetry, as well as several drafts of two novels. Most of her publications have been short nonfiction pieces in regional journals.

James Thurston Davis (2000) is a freelance writer and teacher currently living in Chicago.

Laurin DeChae (2016) is a PhD candidate in Composition & Rhetoric at SUNY Albany, acting as the editor-in-chief of *Barzakh Magazine*. Her work appears or is forthcoming in *Harpur Palate, burntdistrict,* and *Winter Tangerine.* "the sensorium of the cyborg" first appeared in *Pretty Owl Poetry* and was later nominated for possible inclusion in *Best New Poets.* It was also awarded the Phyllis Hurd Liston Poetry Prize and The Academy of American Poets University and College Poetry Prize. "S P E C T A C L E" was previously published in *Animal Literary Magazine.*

Aurielle Destiche (2014 Low Res) is a born and raised San Diegan. Since earning her MFA, she has worked as a copywriter on award-winning projects and continues to write poetry, which she shares on Instagram as @thefreelancepoet.

Gina Ferrara (2008) lives in New Orleans. Her collections include: *The Size of Sparrows* (Finishing Line Press 2006), *Ethereal Avalanche* (Trembling Pillow Press 2009), *Amber Porch Light* (CW Books 2013), *Carville: Amid Moss and Resurrection Fern* (FLP 2014), and *Fitting the Sixth Finger: Poems Inspired by the Paintings of Marc Chagall* was published by Aldrich Press. She teaches English and creative writing at Delgado Community College. Her poetry has appeared in *Callaloo, anderbo, Valley Voices, The Poetry Ireland Review* and others. In 2013 and 2016 she was nominated for a Pushcart. Since

2007 she has curated The Poetry Buffet, a reading series presented by the New Orleans Public Library.

Amelia Cook Fontella (2012 Low Res) is a writer, teacher, and wonderer. She lives in Madison, Wisconsin with her husband Robert Fontella (MFA 2012) and their son Francis. "The Pink Orange" appeared in *Wisconsin People and Ideas* and a version of "Immigrant" appeared in *In Dark and Narrow Spaces.*

Kelly Gartman (2000) was born in Mobile, AL. and moved to New Orleans to attend the MFA program at UNO in 2000. Kelly is currently working on a book of her collected poems & artwork called ANIMAL ME, with a projected publication date of January 2019. When not writing, she's going off on wild new adventures, both planned and unplanned. (Ask her about the wild pigs in Belle Chasse, LA.)

Anne Marie Giovingo (2004).

Jeff Grieneisen (2007 Low Res), a professor of literature and creative writing at State College of Florida, published his first book of poetry, *Good Sumacs*, with MAMMOTH Books; a second manuscript, tentatively titled "Body" is under consideration with another publisher. He was co-founder and associate editor of the annual literary journal *Florida English* for 13 years. In addition to Pound, he has published scholarship on Edgar Allan Poe for Harold Bloom's *Biocritiques* series and the Salem Press Critical Insights Series. His poetry has appeared in many journals and anthologies and has been translated into Portuguese. He has presented his poetry and criticism throughout the U.S. as well as in England, France, Italy, and Scotland. He divides his time between southwest Florida and western Pennsylvania.

Matt Groneman (2011) is an Associate Professor at Vincennes University, a small two-year school in Indiana, where he teaches Creative Writing, Children's Literature, and Composition. When he is not working with students, you can find him reading, listening to music, or playing with his kids.

Kia Groom (2015) is an Australian poet, short fiction writer, and essayist living in New Orleans. Her work has appeared in *Going Down Swinging, Westerly, Overland,* and has been anthologized in *The Hunter Anthology of Contemporary Australian Feminist Poetry* and *Anthology of Western Australian Poetry* (Fremantle Press). She tweets @whodreamedit and can be found at www.kiagroom.com.

Wren Hanks (2016) is the author of *The Rise of Genderqueer*, a 2018 selection for Brain Mill Press's Mineral Point Poetry Series and a finalist for Gold Line Press's chapbook contest. A 2016 Lambda Literary Emerging Writers Fellow, his work has been a finalist for *Indiana Review*'s 2018 1/2 K Prize, anthologized in *Best New Poets*, and recently appears in *Waxwing, Foglifter*, and *Grimoire*. He is also the author of *Prophet Fever* (Hyacinth Girl Press), an Elgin Award finalist, and co-edited *Curious Specimens* (Sundress Publications). He lives in Brooklyn with his wife.

Jade Hurter (2016) is the author of the chapbook *Slut Songs* (Hyacinth Girl Press 2017). She was a finalist in the 2016 Tennessee Williams Poetry Contest, judged by Yusef Komunyakaa, and her recent work appears or is forthcoming in *Passages North, The Columbia Poetry Review, Gingerbread House, New South,* and elsewhere. "The Minotaur" appeared in *The Columbia Poetry Review*; "Still Life" first appeared in *Animal Literary Magazine* and is also included in the chapbook *Slut Songs;* "Leda and the Swan" appeared in *Tinderbox.*

Samantha Isasi (2006) lives in East Tennessee, where she is an Assistant Professor of English and writes.

Kelly Jones (2013). They've taught and tutored at colleges in North Carolina and New Orleans, worked with adult literacy students, led ESOL courses, and been in residence as a communication intern and advisory editor of *I Don't Do Boxes* (a queer southern youth literary magazine) at Elsewhere Museum. Kelly recently earned their Masters in Library and Information Studies, and currently resides in the Piedmont region of North Carolina, where they work as a librarian and arts educator.

Ginny Kaczmarek (2007) is a writer, editor, and critic of literature for both adults and children and is currently the poetry editor for *Literary Mama*. Her publications include *Kirkus Review*, *Women's Review of Books*, *Calyx*, *Rattle*, *The Oxford American*, and the anthology *Birth Writes: A Collection of Real Life Birth Stories*. Recent work has appeared in *Stinkwaves* and *Hypertext*, with more forthcoming from Main Street Rag Press. She lives in New Orleans with her family and blogs at GinnyKaczmarek.com. A slightly different version of "Lament" appeared in the Summer 2008 issue of the *Oxford American*.

Andrew Kindiger (2017) while in the program continued his study of modernism and experimented with writing fiction. He spent a summer in Italy at the Ezra Pound Center for Literature and attended the workshops at University College Cork. The program allowed for the opportunity to tutor in the writing center and to teach briefly at a neighboring university.

Nathaniel Kostar (2017 Low Res) grew up in central New Jersey and has lived and worked in South Korea, Thailand, Europe, and South and Central America. He spent five years in New Orleans fronting a hip-hop/rock band called Tha Neighbors. His first debut album of poetry and hip-hop titled *Love 'n' Travel* is available on https://soundcloud.com/natelost/sets/love-n-travel. He currently lives in Mexico City and hosts ThA Lost Podcast, a series of long-form conversations with artists, trainers, health experts, and interesting people from around the world.

Cathy Lautenbach (2004) works as an artist and freelance editor in Uptown New Orleans.

Jesse Loren (2005 Low Res) is a poet, columnist, non-fiction author and teacher. Jesse is co-editor of *Bombshells: War Stories and Poems by Women on the Homefront*, 2007, and *Mourning Sickness* 2008. Her work can be found in *Exquisite Corpse*, *Yawp*, and *New Virginia Review*. She is a graduate of UC Irvine and currently serves her community as an elected City Councilmember. Her current emphasis is playwriting.

Maya Lowy (2016) was born and raised in Santa Cruz, California, and has been living and writing in New Orleans since 2013. Her poems can be found in *The Golden Key, Quaint Magazine, The Maple Leaf Rag, FOCI Arts Magazine, Kalyna Review,* and other publications. "Wurstfest, New Braunfels, 11/9/2016" appeared in *States of the Union.*

Matthew C. Mackey (2012 Low Res) managed Buried Letter Press, an independent arts and criticism magazine, for five years but left his post to take a South American sojourn. Thankfully, for some, he has returned. Currently, he digs around in the Rockies dreaming of gold when he has the time. Otherwise, he can be found lurking around Denver, Colorado. Of course, he writes and reads and misses his friends and family from time to time. He hopes to see them soon.

Jana Mackin (2006) is a poet and journalist who spends her time between Wallace, Idaho, and Wilmington, North Carolina.

Whitney Mackman (2013) is an adjunct at Tulane University and Xavier University. She is a writer, lacrosse umpire, and adventure specialist who dreams of living in a tree house and mountain biking all over the world. During the summer, she is a mountain bike coach for a nonprofit in Boulder, CO. She earned a B.A. in English from the University of Puget Sound in Tacoma, Washington.

j.s. makkos (2006) is a writer, designer, and printer living in New Orleans. As an archivist he actively curates Nola DNA, a rare collection of thousands of historic newspapers.

Jesse Manley (2010) attended exactly one graduate class in UNO's Creative Writing Workshop before having to evacuate for Hurricane Katrina. Coming back was one of the most questionable decisions he's ever made, yet easily the most fruitful. He is an editor emeritus of *Bayou Magazine* and *Ellipsis*, but his proudest accomplishment at UNO was wrangling three readers a month for the Gold Room graduate reading series for three years. He has taught at UNO, Dillard, and now teaches at Nicholls State University, where UNO CWW graduates have taken over almost half the English department. His work has appeared in *The Rio Grande Review, Words and Images, The Extrovert, Burlesque Press, The Brazos Review*, and *Bigger Than They Appear: Anthology of Very Short Poems.* "Today, I Threw Out Your Toothbrush" appeared in *The Rio Grande Review* (2010) and *Bigger Than They Appear: Anthology of Very Short Poems* (2011).

Dawn Manning (2012 Low Res) is the author of *Postcards from the Dead Letter Office*. In addition to receiving the Beullah Rose Poetry Prize and a subsequent Pushcart nomination, her poems have been awarded the San Miguel Poetry Prize, the Edith Garlow Poetry Prize, and many honors. Her poems have been published through *American Poetry Journal, Crab Orchard Review, Smartish Pace*, and other literary journals. She is a Mona Van Duyn Scholar to the 2017 Sewanee Writers' Conference. Most days you can find her at her favorite anvil wielding a hammer and torch. When the stars align, she travels. "Juanita" appeared in *Other Countries: Contemporary Poets Rewiring History (*United Kingdom: Inpress (2014) and in *Creative Crossroads of the Americas*, Mexico: 14, January, 2013. "Fables from the Petrified Forest" appeared in *Smartish Pace* 22 (2015). "Burning the Bodies" appeared in *Silk Road* 14 (2015).

Jim McCormick (1994) is a two-time Grammy nominated, multi-platinum songwriter who has celebrated two #1 songs on the Billboard country charts: Jason Aldean's "Take A Little Ride," which spent 3-weeks at the top, and Brantley Gilbert's "You Don't Know Her Like I Do." His songs have also been recorded by Tim McGraw, Keith Urban, Kelly Clarkson, Luke Bryan, Harry Connick Jr., Smash Mouth, Jon Pardi, Trisha Yearwood, Randy Travis, Charlie Pride, Kristin Chenowith, Ronnie Milsap, Trace Adkins, Jamey Johnson, Shenandoah, and the Write Brothers. A native of New Orleans, McCormick holds a bachelor's degree from Georgetown University.

Jessica Morey-Collins (2016) is a Pushcart and Best of the Net nominated poet and educator. She won an Academy of American Poets award and worked as associate poetry editor for *Bayou Magazine*. Her poems and essays can be found in *Pleiades, The Pinch, Juked, Animal Literary Journal* and elsewhere. She is currently working on a Masters of Community and Regional Planning at the University of Oregon. "TASTE" appeared in *The North American Review;* "SUPPOSE LONELINESS" appeared in *Whiskey Island;* "DIRT HEART" appeared in *The Fem.*

Jackson Moss (2006) received his MFA the first full semester after Katrina. It was also during that grim and acrid time of gutted houses and fetid fridges that he began to write about politics and sports for *NOLAFugees.* Nowadays, when not golfing or gambling, he is at Delgado Community College, where he serves as the Assistant Department Chair of English. He enjoys teaching the Greco-Roman classics, as well as the works of Dante and Chaucer. Robert Frost and Alan Dugan remain his favorite American poets, and his favorite weapon is his putter, Zenyatta.

Allyson Nobles (2017 Low Res) is a New Orleans native who attended the New Orleans Center for Creative Arts in Jazz Piano. She has a Bachelor of Arts in Music Studies and English from the University of New Orleans. She is currently based in New York City but can normally be found on a sailboat, plane, or in her car on the road.

Adam Peltz (2004) works with medical students in Tulane University's Department of Family and Community Medicine. He lives with his wife, Ashley Miner, their fraternal twin daughters, and their two cats in the Marigny, near the Press Street railroad tracks and the Mississippi River in New Orleans. Some of his poems have appeared in a handful of journals, including *South Carolina Review, Platte Valley Review* (edited by Robert Ficociello, a UNO alumnus), *A Bad Penny Review* (edited by Johnny Damm, a UNO alumnus), and *2River View.*

Ann Plicque (2010) won the Vassar Miller and Andrea Gereighty Saunders poetry prizes. She has a B.A. in journalism and has written screenplays. Ann is a Body Pump coach and believes a healthy body keeps the mind sharp. She has been a Strategy Consultant with the Energy Wise Alliance, a program that encourages energy conservation and helps people insulate homes. She recently won the Associated Writer's Mentor/Mentee Award and is at work on completing a poetry manuscript with a professional poet and teacher who is her mentor. She hopes to earn a PhD in Creative Writing in poetry and linguistics in the near future. Ann is a native New Orleanian and finds her home is her poetry, her poetry her home.

Sarah Rae (2013 Low Res) lives in Chicago with her cat Maya, and has worked as a high school counselor and English teacher. Her poems and translations have appeared in Burlesque Press, *fieralingue, Solamente en San Miguel, Revista Blanca y Negro, Tata Nacho* Press, and *Ezra*, among others.

Beverly Rainbolt (2000) wrote a few poems and got a few of them published. But most of all she got to hang around with the coolest of kids who live and breathe to explore their worlds—inner, outer, natural and made up—for the simple purpose of spilling those worlds letter by letter by space into words into lines into brilliance to share. For that she is grateful. Her book, *The Altar of This Moment*, was published by Portals Press (2001) in which "The Text is Dead—Long Live the Text" and "Forest Park West" appeared. "Forest Park West" was reprinted in *World of Women Poets* (Red Hen Press, 2008).

Trisha Rezende (2008) hails from the island nation of Trinidad and Tobago. She has taught Composition, Creative Writing, and/or Poetry classes at Dillard University and UNO. She currently teaches at Xavier University. Her poetry has been published in *Poet Lore, Burlesque Press, FLARE*, and *Blackstone Review.*

Brenda Nettles Riojas (2012 Low Res) is the host of *Corazón Bilingüe*, a weekly radio program featuring interviews with writers, which airs on 88.1/88.9 FM, a local NPR affiliate in the Rio Grande Valley in South Texas. *La Primera Voz Que Oí* is her first collection of Spanish poetry and a collection of persona poems is due out by Slough Press in the fall. Her work has been published in a variety of publications including *New Border Voices: An Anthology.* A journalist and columnist, Brenda is currently the Director of Communications for the Diocese of Brownsville, where she also serves as the editor of *The Valley Catholic* newspaper.

Spencer Silverthorne (2016) is a poet from Southeastern Pennsylvania. He earned a BA in English from Kenyon College in 2007. He was a resident at the Vermont Studio Center. Currently, he teaches English in rural South Africa. His poems have appeared in *Pelican Bomb, Title-Magazine,* and others. "MOST ELIGIBLE BACHELOR: FRANK OCEAN" and "THE SPEAKER'S HISTORY OF KISSING" appeared in *Assaracus;* "THE SPEAKER CAN'T BE IN THIS POEM" appeared in *Unbroken.*

Sophia Stone (1995) was a member of the first MFA class at the University of New Orleans. She spent twelve years as an editor of the *New Orleans Review*, including six years as poetry editor. She has lived in Vermont since 2006. "An Expressionist Painting" appeared in *New Orleans Review;* "Leaving a Freshman at College" appeared in *The Southern Review;* "Flying" appeared in *The North American Review.*

Kat Stromquist (2013). Her poems have appeared in numerous literary journals; she received the Maxine & Joseph Cassin Prize for best thesis in poetry, Penumbra's Carducci Prize, and second prize in the Mississippi Valley Poetry contest. She works as a journalist.

Diane Vance (1998). Her work has appeared in *The North American Review, The Southwestern Review*, and the anthologies *My Lover is a Woman* (Ballantine Books), *Women Poets Workshop Into Print* (In(her)itance Press) and *Letters to the World* (Red Hen Press).

Lauren Walter (2016) grew up in Brookfield, Wisconsin until the age of twelve and then lived in Dixon, Illinois. She received her Bachelor of Arts in English from the University of New Orleans in 2013. Currently, she works in digital marketing.

Patricia A. Ward (1998), an African-American, was born in New Orleans, Louisiana on September 11, 1938. Ward was educated in the public schools of New Orleans. Education was encouraged by her parents. She earned a B. A. from Southern University at New Orleans and Teacher Certification from Tulane University. While a teacher at Eleanor McMain Magnet School, she traveled to West

Africa as a Fulbright-Hays scholar. Her poems have appeared in the anthology *A Bend in the River, Xavier Review,* and *three poets in new orleans.* Currently, she volunteers at People Program of New Orleans, a nonprofit organization that offers classes to people fifty years and older where she conducts a poetry class.

Tara Waudby (2014 Low Res) is passionate about innovation in education and is committed to increasing meaning and relevance in schools. She began her teaching career in Phoenix, Arizona before moving into international education. She also holds an MA in Educational Leadership and a graduate certificate in educational technology. Her research interests include building compassionate school cultures, digital literacy, and systems development. Currently, she volunteers for ISTE as the Chair Elect of the Digital Storytelling Network, for COETAIL as a learning coach, and for NESA as a member of the Professional Development Advisory Committee. Through her blog "consider another truth", she explores the gray matter of education.

Clare Welsh (2017) is an artist, writer, and photographer based in New Orleans. Her drawings have appeared on the covers of books and magazines, and her writing can be found in *Offbeat Magazine, Pressure Life, Salt, Southern Glossary,* among others. For a detailed portfolio, check out her website at http://clarewelsh.format.com.

Kelcy Wilburn (2010) has published in *Waccamaw*, *Hobart*, and *Big Lucks*, among other journals. Professionally and creatively, she splits her time between writing and music and, under the name Kelcy Mae, has released two full-length albums since graduating from the CWW. Based in New Orleans, she tours nationally and has another project forthcoming in 2018. (KelcyMae.com) "Though We May Not Discuss" appeared in *Waccamaw.*

Deborah Brink Wöhrmann (2004 Low Res) lives in Portland, Oregon with her husband and dog, writing, gardening, cooking, hiking, and leading the occasional poetry workshop. Also a body-worker, she marvels at the mind's impact on how we move and feel, and the body's ability to wake the spirit and alter our way of seeing and being.

FACULTY

John Gery's seven collections of poetry include *The Enemies of Leisure* (1995), *Davenport's Version* (2003), *A Gallery of Ghosts*, (2008), *Lure* (2011), and *Have at You Now!* (2014). His work has appeared in journals throughout the U.S., as well as in the U.K. and Canada, and he has been translated into seven languages. Gery has received fellowships from the NEA, the Fulbright Foundation, the Louisiana Division of the Arts, and the University of Minnesota Center for Advanced Studies, among others. Gery has also published criticism on poets ranging from Ezra Pound and H.D. to Amiri Baraka, John Ashbery, and Marilyn Chin, as well as the critical work, *Nuclear Annihilation and Contemporary American Poetry: Ways of Nothingness* (1996). With Rosella Mamoli Zorzi, Massimo Bacigalupo, and Stefano Maria Casella, he co-authored *In Venice and the Veneto with Ezra Pound* (2007), and with Vahe Baladouni, he wrote the biography, *Hmayeak Shems: A Poet of Pure Spirit* (2010). He has also edited four books of poetry and criticism and has worked as a collaborative translator from Serbian, Italian, Chinese, Armenian and French.

A Research Professor of English and member of the Women and Gender Studies faculty at UNO, Gery has been teaching at UNO since 1979. He also directs the Ezra Pound Center for Literature (EPCL), Brunnenburg, Italy, which conducts summer seminars in Creative Writing and Pound's work at the castle of Pound's family in northern Italy. Since 2005 he has served as Secretary of the Ezra Pound International Conference and is Series Editor for the EPCL Book Series at Clemson University Press. He has lectured and read poems throughout the U.S., as well as in Italy, Serbia, Spain, China, South Korea, and the U.K. He lives in New Orleans with his wife, poet Biljana Obradovic, and their son, Petar Gery. "American Ghost" and "The Enemies of Leisure" from *The Enemies of Leisure* (Story Line Press). Copyright © 1995 by John Gery. From *A Pack of Lies*: "Lie #4: That Frances Osgood Slept with E.A. Poe" and "Stump" from *A Gallery of Ghosts* (University of New Orleans Press). Copyright © 2008 by John Gery. "Lag Time" and "Spring Offensive" from *Have at You Now!* (CW Books). Copyright 2014 by John Gery. "Spring Offensive" originally appeared in *Poets Against the War*, Ed.

Sam Hamill with Sally Anderson and others (Nation Books, 2003). "Paratextual Saxophone" originally appeared in *Improbable Worlds: An Anthology of Texas and Louisiana Poets*. Ed. Martha Serpas (Mutabilis Press, 2011). Other poems appear here for the first time.

Carolyn Hembree was born in Bristol, Tennessee. Her debut poetry collection, *Skinny*, came out from Kore Press in 2012. In 2016, Trio House Books published her second collection, *Rigging a Chevy into a Time Machine and Other Ways to Escape a Plague*, selected by Neil Shepard for the 2015 Trio Award and by Stephanie Strickland for the 2015 Rochelle Ratner Memorial Award. Her work has appeared in *Colorado Review*, *Gulf Coast*, *Indiana Review*, *Poetry Daily*, and other publications. She received a 2016-2017 ATLAS grant from the Louisiana Board of Regents and has also received grants and fellowships from PEN, the Louisiana Division of the Arts, and the Southern Arts Federation. Carolyn teaches at the University of New Orleans and serves as poetry editor of *Bayou Magazine*.

Bill Lavender (1995) is a poet, novelist, musician, and carpenter. He worked at UNO as Coordinator of Study Abroad Programs in Writing from 1998 until 2013, when he "retired." He also served as the Low Residency MFA Program's first Graduate Coordinator beginning in 2000. In 2006, he also took over the Directorship of UNO Press. Since "retiring" he has devoted his attention to Lavender Ink, a small press devoted mainly to poetry, which he founded in 1995, and its new imprint *Diálogos*, which is devoted to literatures of cross cultural significance, mostly in translation.

He is the author of seven full-length books and numerous poems, stories and essays in chapbooks and print and web journals and anthologies. His verse memoir, *Memory Wing*, called by Rodger Kamenetz "a contemporary autobiographical masterpiece," was published by Black Widow in 2011. His novel, *Q*, a neo-picaresque view of our late-capitalist utopia, appeared from Trembling Pillow Press in 2013. A chapbook, *surrealism*, was published in 2016 by Lavender Ink. The Spring 2017 issue of *Xavier Review* presents a retrospective of his work. He is the co-founder, with Megan Burns, of the New Orleans Poetry Festival. "A Writers' Retreat (Marginalia)" will appear in a forthcoming publication, *My ID*.

Kay Murphy (Goddard College, 1980) is Professor Emerita at the University of New Orleans where she taught in the English Department, the Creative Writing Workshop, the Honors Program, and served as Poetry Editor for *Bayou*. She was awarded the Louisiana Division of the Arts Individual Artist Grant for her poetry and a University-wide Excellence in Teaching Award. During her tenure at UNO (1984-2010) she has published over fifty essay/reviews of contemporary poetry in national journals such as *The American Book Review*, *Chelsea*, and *The Spoon River Poetry Review*. Besides reviews, she has published fiction in such journals as *Ascent* and *Fiction International*. Her heart-genre, poetry, has appeared in over 100 journals such as *North American Review*, *Mississippi Review*, *Poetry*, *Painted Bride Quarterly*, and *College English*. She is the author of two poetry collections: *The Autopsy* and *Belief Blues*. Her third collection, *Soul Tooth* is looking for a publisher. She has taught in Innsbruck, Austria, Montpellier, France, San Miguel, Mexico, Edinburgh, Scotland, and Cork, Ireland. "My Mother Calls Me" and "Undiagnosed Villanelle" appeared in *Painted Bride Quarterly*. "On *El Día de Los Muertos* Neruda Speaks to Me" appeared in *Poetic Voices Without Borders*. The Neruda line "Hurl yourself into your grief like a dove, like snow on the dead" is the last line in a section of his "From: The Woes and The Furies" inspired by Quevedo's line *In my heart are the woes and the furies*, which Neruda uses as an epigraph.